THE GUY'S GUIDE TO THE ENNEAGRAM

The Guy's Guide to the Enneagram

A New Way to Understand and Apply the Enneagram at Work and at Home

Nick Shell & Ramon Presson

Franklin, TN

Published by Ramon Presson

Printed in the United States of America

DEDICATIONS

From Nick

Dedicated to with apologies to my wife, my kids, my parents, my sister, my friends, and any innocent bystanders at the grocery store who encountered me testing out my Enneagram theories on them in preparation for writing this book.

From Ramon

Dedicated to my wife, Dorrie, who is my in-home Enneagram expert and coach, my favorite Type 2 on the planet, and simply the best person I know.

Contents

Part I. Getting Yourself Ready for the Game

1. Our Pregame Speech   3

2. The Enneagram in Your Closest Relationship   23

Part II. Identifying Your Position on the Field

3. Type 1: The Self-Criticizing Reformer   33

4. Type 2: The Self-Denying Hidden Warrior   45

5. Type 3: The Self-Shaming Achiever   59

6. Type 4: The Self-Conscious Innovator   69

7. Type 5: The Self-Sufficient Minimalist   79

8. Type 6: The Self-Doubting Troubleshooter   91

9. Type 7: The Self-Driven Variety Seeker   103

10. Type 8: The Self-Reliant Challenger   115

11. Type 9: The Self-Erasing Negotiator   127

Part III. Deepening Insights About Your Role

12. "Wait, What's a Wing?" A Brief Dictionary of   145
     Enneagram Terms

13. Going Deeper in the Types   169

14. Some Thoughts about the Three Emotions   187

15. Guys Like Us   193

16. Recommended Resources for Further Study   197

More by Nick Shell and Ramon Presson   201

Part I

Getting Yourself Ready for the Game

I

OUR PREGAME SPEECH

———————

"Only the shallow really know themselves." –Oscar Wilde

"I've lived with me 24/7 every single day of my entire life, and yet I'm still a mystery to me." – Ramon Presson

From Ramon:

Winston Churchill was speaking about the difficulty of predicting the future actions of Russia at the end of World War II when he said, "It is a riddle, wrapped in mystery, inside an enigma, but perhaps there is a key."

If you're anything like me, you also feel like a riddle wrapped in mystery inside an enigma. How often have you said to yourself, "Why did I do that? How did that come out of my mouth? What in the world was I thinking?"

Akin to the lists of The Seven Natural Wonders of the World and The Seven (Man-Made) Wonders of the World, you can go online and read about The Seven Unsolved Mysteries of the World. Truth be told, we could all nominate ourselves as the Great Eighth Unsolved Mystery.

In one of the closing scenes of the film, *Titanic*, Rose says, "A woman's heart is a deep ocean of secrets." And that is likely true. And it is most likely true of men as well. We all have secrets that few know or that no one knows and that we will never tell.

But there are secrets hidden even from ourselves. And not just the kind of secrets that our subconscious holds and guards, so inaccessible that they might as well be stored in another galaxy. Rather, I'm referring to the secret and mysterious parts of ourselves that are hiding just around the corner of our awareness.

In a *Psychology Today* article regarding self-awareness, Dr. Tchiki Davis writes, "Quite frankly, most of us are running on autopilot, hardly aware of why we succeed or fail, or why we behave as we do. Our minds are so busy with daily chatter that we usually only self-reflect when something goes awfully wrong."

Indeed, it seems that the journey to self-awareness remains one of the most elusive quests for most of us, often leaving us trapped in patterns of self-defeat.

In an article for the *Harvard Business Review*, Dr Tasha Eurich said, "Even though most people *believe* they are self-aware, only 10%—15% of the people we studied actually fit the criteria."

Aren't you often a mystery to yourself? Don't you find yourself asking...

- "Why did I do that?"

- "Why does that bother me so much?"

- "Am I the only one here thinking this way?"
- "Where did that reaction come from?

Personality History

The study of personality has from its beginning sought to solve the mysteries of human behavior and motives. Personality researchers are like detectives looking for clues at the scene of the crime. And what's the crime? It's that we humans often don't seem to make sense.

Interest in individual personality predates even the fathers and founders of psychology. Greek physician Hippocrates (460-370 BC) believed that human personality, moods, and behavior are influenced by one of four dominant bodily fluids leading them to have one of the four corresponding temperaments—phlegmatic, sanguine, melancholic, and choleric.

Fast forward and every model of human psychology had/has its own theories as to the source and cause of individual personality and the number of different personality types or traits it proposed. Currently, the most popular and most widely used models of personality are the Myers-Briggs-Type Indicator, the DiSC, and the Enneagram.

Why I'm an Advocate of the Enneagram

Personally, I am an advocate and fan of the Enneagram, thus the desire to collaborate with Nick Shell on this book. I've found the Enneagram to be accurate, flexible, and user-friendly in offering insights for my personal growth as well as providing a better understanding of others, particularly those closest to me. That increased understanding of self and others leads to improved communication and ultimately to healthier relationships.

My wife, Dorrie, is a certified and highly experienced career coach and an expert in the Enneagram's applications for personal growth, relational enrichment, and professional/leadership/team development. We discovered that when both of us understood our own Enneagram personality type as well as each other's primary type the level of helpful insight for our relationship was multiplied by four! We came to refer to it as "Insight to the 4th power" if you vaguely recall exponential numbers in math class.

However, my first impression of the Enneagram wasn't so positive. When I first encountered the Enneagram many years ago from just the cover of a book on the shelf of a Barnes & Noble, the word "Enneagram" itself along with the established graphic for it gave me pause.

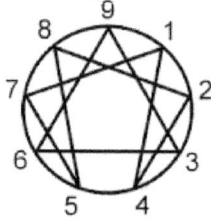

My first thought was "What kind of weird New Age thing is *that?*" I didn't even pick up the book and look through it.

Fast forward a decade, and shortly before Ian Cron came out with his bestselling Enneagram primer, *The Road Back to You*, I heard Richard Rohr, whom I respect, mention the Enneagram in an interview, and this time it intrigued me. (It turns out that it was

Rohr's book on the shelf that weirded me out a decade earlier. I didn't know who he was at that time.)

Since the release of Cron's first book and his co-author Suzanne Stabile's book, *The Path Between Us,* curiosity about and interest in the Enneagram has soared. Enneagram books, articles, podcasts, social media posts, videos, webinars, conferences, and workshops have exploded onto the scene.

Hidden in Plain Sight

It's fascinating to observe something as old and as well-established as the Enneagram be discovered by a new generation. But despite the increased awareness and popularity of the Enneagram, many people...

a) have not heard of the Enneagram

b) have heard of it but don't know what it is and are curious

c) have heard of it, don't understand it, and are skeptical of it as a passing fad

d) have heard of it, don't understand it, and are suspicious about it

A few years ago, I kept thinking, "I wish there was a way to make the Enneagram seem more user-friendly to the curious, the skeptical, and the suspicious." One day it dawned on me that the Nine Types could be thought of as the nine positions on a baseball field. And I began playing around with sketches that ultimately became the baseball diamond graphic you see.

See The Field and Play Your Position
A New Way to Understand and Apply the Enneagram

One of the truths inherent in the metaphor of the baseball diamond is the reminder that all the positions matter and are important for a team to succeed. No Enneagram type is inherently better or is more important than any other type. A community needs all the types. That's important to keep in mind as you learn about the Enneagram and specifically your type.

Before embarking upon the writing of this book I asked myself the following questions...

- *Honestly, does the world really need another Enneagram book?*

- *And if not, then what would my book contribute to the available knowledge and current abundance of books about the Enneagram? In other words, why bother?*

This was my answer: This book would introduce the Enneagram to a segment of the population, especially guys, who are either completely unaware of the Enneagram or who are currently dismissing it as a relevant and helpful resource.

Why an Enneagram Book for Guys?

Here's a fact that all published authors are aware of and all publishers certainly know. Women buy and read more books than men, including more books on personal growth and relationship books. At one time men were the predominant buyers of professional growth and business development books but any significant sales gap between men and women in that market no longer exists. Hence, a corresponding fact is that more women know about the Enneagram and know their Enneagram type than do men. More women than men are thus effectively applying the Enneagram to personal and professional development and to improvement in their professional and personal relationships. It's not a competition, but the truth is that men lag behind women in being intentional about self-understanding.

Therefore, what you have here is a user-friendly book about the Enneagram written *by* two guys *for* guys.

Brian Herbert writes, "The capacity to learn is a gift. The ability to learn is a skill. The willingness to learn is a choice." As the authors, it is our hope that you will make the choice to seize the gift and skill of learning, and may this book be just a small part of that lifelong journey of growth.

Our Invitation to Women

Ladies, there is zero intent to exclude you by writing this book with men in mind. In fact, we invite you to read this book to better understand a significant man in your life—father, brother, boyfriend, husband, son, son-in-law, father-in-law, co-worker, boss, etc. Plus, as a side benefit, you'll learn something about yourself when reading any good book about the Enneagram, regardless of who is its target audience.

From 2011 to 2014, Nick was *Parents* magazine's official Daddy Blogger, with his popular blog, *The Dadabase*. Based on the reader stats and responses, Nick learned that the overwhelming majority of his readers on that national platform were not actually dads. Instead, they were moms, who apparently were trying to understand the mysterious male mind of their husband and the father of their children.

So, ladies, we're glad you've picked up this book, and we hope you find in it some ideas and truths that are helpful to you in better understanding our species, more specifically the one in your home.

We hope that you'll consider gifting the book to one of those significant men in your life. By the way, never give a book to a man and say, "Here, you need to read this." That will sound to him like an assignment from a teacher or a prescription from a psychiatrist, and it's probably the surest way to guarantee he doesn't read it. Your best bet is to say something like, "Hey, I found this book written by two guys, and it looks interesting. I'd be curious about some of your impressions after you've read a little bit when you have time. Not being a guy, I don't know if they're on target or not, so I'd be interested in your thoughts."

Guys, if your wife has brought this book to your attention, thank her. It means she cares. I'm aware that your first inclination might be to say something like, "You're always assigning me books to read," or "You're always trying to change me." Please don't say that. Immediately shooting down someone's curiosity, interest, or idea like it's a clay pigeon in a skeet shooting contest is very demoralizing and frustrating. You've undoubtedly had the experience of having your intentions and motives doubted and have had an interest or idea quickly dismissed or criticized. It doesn't feel good, does it? So, don't do it to her. And if you do (or did), then apologize.

My Invitation to Nick

In full disclosure, the majority of chapters in this book, specifically much of the nine chapters devoted to describing the nine Enneagram types have been written by my friend, Nick Shell. In presenting the idea for this book to Nick I said the following to him in an email:

Nick, I thought about you and am reaching out to you about this book project because...

- I'd rather co-author this project with someone than do it alone. I believe I would enjoy the process more, and the end product will be better if I collaborate with someone. Plus, the book is more likely to actually get completed and make it out into the world if I don't work alone on it.

- Nick, you are very knowledgeable about the Enneagram and passionate about it as a tool that can help people in personal, spiritual, and relational growth.

- You are a creative and innovative thinker and a very good writer.

- I know you and I trust you.

Sidenote to Men: As a male only child, I tend to be independent and self-sufficient. The mantra I naturally lean toward is, "I'll figure it out. I'll take care of it. I'll get it done." Add to that inclination, I'm an Enneagram Type 2 (which you'll learn more about later in the book) which among other things, means I'm much more comfortable offering help than requesting help or receiving help.

In recent years, especially after reading an outstanding book by business leader Dan Sullivan and psychologist Dr Benjamin Hardy titled *Who, Not How* which demonstrates the advantages of collaboration over solo efforts, I have made a shift in my thinking about requesting feedback, asking for help, delegation, outsourcing, and collaboration. Note that the Sullivan & Hardy book itself is a collaboration between the two men, and they briefly share their reasons and process for the collaboration.

I mention this for two reasons:

- I want you to know right up-front that while the idea for this book was mine, the heavy lifting has been done by Nick. If a book idea and outline is a skeleton, then Nick has done the harder work of creating and adding organs, muscles, ligaments, tissue, and skin. He's solely responsible for crafting the nine chapters covering the nine Enneagram types. You'll see where I pop up briefly with some thoughts about Type 2s and Type 9s in those dedicated chapters.

- Most men are like me, inclined to independence and self-sufficiency when it comes to getting things done. You don't have to be an only child or an Enneagram 2 to prefer riding solo than on a tandem bike when it comes to productivity. Note that this has nothing to do with being sociable, friendly, or a good team player. It simply means that as a guy, admitting your need for help and asking for help is not your default response to projects or problems.

This leads me to make two statements and ask you two questions. It's a slight detour from the Enneagram, but as I often say with a grin to my patients during a therapy session, "I'm giving you this next piece of profound wisdom for free. No extra charge."

1. **Problems:** I urge you to admit your need for assistance and be willing to ask for it. Your soul, your marriage, and your water heater cannot always be fixed by watching a YouTube video.

Question: Is there a problem you are currently making worse by denying it, ignoring it, or by trying to figure it out and fix it on your own?

2. **Projects:** I exhort you not to fall for the myth of "If you want something done right, you have to do it yourself." Instead, improve the quality of completed projects by asking for help or by enlisting collaboration. This book is a tangible representation of this axiom. This book is not only better because of Nick's involvement, it wouldn't even exist without his involvement.

By the way, you'll likely be able to tell which one of us is writing which parts because Nick and I have different writing styles, and we've intentionally embraced that difference in the writing of this book versus A) either of us trying to write more like the other person, or B) trying to merge our two styles into a third composite version that would barely sound like either one of us.

Question: What project is taking longer than it should OR hasn't even gotten started because you are determined to figure it out and do it yourself?

Alright, now that I got that out of my system, let's get back to the Enneagram...

From Nick:

There is a rumor that I am obsessed with the Enneagram. It might even be true that my wife and kids are now fully accustomed to me initiating conversations with random strangers any time we leave the house and ultimately drive the conversation to me helping them understand themselves, due to me revealing to them which Enneagram type they show signs of being.

Not only have I spent much of my time as a certified Enneagram coach, including running a YouTube channel on the subject, I have read all the other Enneagram books, so you don't have to.

You'll see me reference them throughout the upcoming chapters. Consider our book both a prequel as well as a sequel to all other Enneagram books out there on the market.

How to Read This Book

The reality is that while we have a dominant personality type, we are all a combination of the nine types. Every one of us is a unique blend of the nine types. No one is 100% of one type or 0% percent of one type. We exhibit facets of those personality types throughout the course of the day— or in my case, in the course of any given hour.

So instead of focusing on just one Enneagram type, we are inviting you to see how all nine types actually apply and how they express themselves in you and through you.

Specifically, we invite you to read this book out of order. I can assure you, that's how I (Nick) wrote the middle nine chapters on the Types, starting with the Enneagram numbers I relate to most.

For example, if you think you might be an Enneagram 5, then make that the first chapter you read, as a means of helping to confirm that you really are a 5. Then from there, choose another Enneagram number that seems the most interesting to you.

I say this because if you're like me, you didn't luck out and figure out your Enneagram by taking just one free online assessment. In fact, I've taken a dozen Enneagram tests and they were not consistent across the board in accurately identifying my type.

The reason? We often see ourselves from a certain perspective or concept of who we think we are in the world, whether it's an avatar of who we aspire to become, or possibly even a lesser version of ourselves because we happen to be in stress mode on that particular day.

Another surprising curveball can be when a person is a more introverted or more extroverted version of an Enneagram type that is more well-known for being the opposite.

Even if you are convinced you already know your Enneagram type, I urge you to be open to the possibility that your type was misdiagnosed. This is a lesson I know from experience... about eight different times!

Ask any of my family members about how many times my

Enneagram type "changed." It even became a running joke, "Alright Nick, which Enneagram number are you this week?"

If nothing else, the trial-and-error method of discovering my actual Enneagram type, which meant I was wrong multiple times over the course of the few years it took me to figure out my true self underneath all of my alter egos, revealed I definitely am not an Enneagram 3... because clearly, I don't fear failure!

Being "wrong" is simply another opportunity to learn.

I tell you this because I want you to give yourself the same freedom to "be wrong" about who you think you are. One of the most fascinating things about the Enneagram is that it helps to uncover and reveal what is actually going on inside of our psyche.

In the midst of the constant war of logical checkpoints versus emotional decisions we deal with each day, there is a solid, yet subconscious, operating system which serves as a predictable force as it dictates how we react to those logical checkpoints and emotional decisions.

It reminds me of those familiar treasure map episodes of Saturday morning cartoon shows in the 1980s and 1990s I watched when I was a kid. The entire plot was driven by a group of kids/ Smurfs/Muppet Babies trying to find the hidden golden treasure, based on a map they somehow got their hands on.

Of course, it always ended with the characters opening an empty chest with nothing but a note in the bottom, proclaiming that the real treasure had been inside their hearts all along, and that the journey itself helped them to realize that. That serves as a good analogy of how the Enneagram works.

Once you discover your Enneagram number, you can't help but look back at your entire life and see all the otherwise obscure nuances through the lens of a reformer, a helper, a performer, an individualist, an investigator, a loyalist, an enthusiast, a challenger, or a mediator. The light will come on. There are things that will make sense. You'll have "Aha" moments when you connect some dots between your childhood experiences and your adult personality.

As Ramon has shown, a way to illustrate the nine unique personalities of the Enneagram is via the nine positions out on the field for a baseball team.

Enneagram 1: The Reformer as the pitcher
Enneagram 2: The Helper as the catcher
Enneagram 3: The Performer as the 1st baseman
Enneagram 4: The Individualist as the 2nd baseman
Enneagram 5: The Investigator as the shortstop
Enneagram 6: The Loyalist as the 3rd baseman
Enneagram 7: The Enthusiast as the left fielder
Enneagram 8: The Challenger as center fielder
Enneagram 9: The Mediator as right fielder

By the way, don't make too much of the connection between a certain position on the field and its corresponding Enneagram type. The Mediator could just as easily be the shortstop in this diagram. There's no special significance that the 1st baseman is a Performer or that a Helper is behind the plate.

Typing Lessons

While it is important to discover your main Enneagram type, it is just as vital to take a journey though all nine types since all nine are connected and are a part of what makes you, you.

As I (Nick) take you through each chapter assigned to each

Enneagram type, I will be focusing on several men whom I have known personally for years. It's important to know what an actual real-life man looks like as each Enneagram, beyond simply using caricatures of what we have been taught that each number is supposed to look like.

For example, most Enneagram 4 males are not as eccentric as The Artist Formerly Known as Prince.

Now that introductions have been made along with some explanations and some recommendations for getting the most out of this book, let's jump in. Or perhaps we should say...PLAY BALL!

Your Personality Type is Not a Pigeonhole

Charles Schulz once revealed in an interview that his *Peanuts* characters represented different aspects of himself—the philosophical and spiritual Linus, critical and crabby Lucy, carefree and imaginative Snoopy, and melancholic and self-doubting Charlie Brown. Those cartoon characters each reflect an aspect of Schulz's own personality. But it was Charlie Brown, "the loveable loser" with whom Schulz felt the deepest personal connection. Schulz spoke of not being athletic or good-looking as a teenager, feeling plain and insecure. And despite his success as the creator of one of the most beloved comic strips of all-time, Schulz confessed that he still battled insecurity as a mature adult.

As I remind my individual therapy patients and couples, no one is just completely one personality type. There are no full-blooded Enneagram 5s, no 100% ENFPs, no pure-bred high Ds. All of us are like red wine blends versus a pure chardonnay or merlot from a single species of grape.

However, in our personality blend we each do have a dominant or more prevalent type that shows up in how we think, what we feel, what we value, and how we act and react. For Charles Schulz, while Charlie Brown represented just one aspect of his complete personality, it was the aspect with the most influence.

Keep the Goal in Mind

When exploring the Enneagram and your Enneagram type you will get the most out of your study by being humble and honest with yourself about your personality type's strengths and weaknesses. Another way to think of it is that your personality type has three versions on a continuum of sorts: an unhealthy version, a standard version, and a healthy version. Your desire and goal should be to become the healthiest version of you. Being the healthiest version of you will be of great benefit to you and of benefit to those with whom you are in close relationship with.

Neither the need nor goal is to change your personality and switch to another personality because there is nothing wrong with your core personality. No personality type is better or worse than any other personality type. Each has its bright spots and its shadow sides. This is why I like to think of the nine Enneagram personality types like the nine positions on a baseball field. All nine positions on the diamond are valuable and needed.

Acceptance and Adjustment

One of the reasons I'm such a proponent of Enneagram work is that I believe it is an excellent tool to increase self-understanding, and with that self-understanding you can then engage what I call the "creative tension between Acceptance and Adjustment."

Through having a greater understanding of my personality I'm in a better position to accept myself. But healthy acceptance doesn't mean complacency. Healthy acceptance says, "I don't need to become someone else. However, what meaningful and reasonable adjustments can I make to be the best version of myself?"

Do you see that creative tension? If I overemphasize Acceptance I'm at risk of personal complacency and laziness, of minimizing and justifying bad attitudes and behavior, and making excuses for the inexcusable because "this is just who I am." As a therapist I hear people do this all the time, excusing behavior because they're Irish/German/Italian/Latino, or because they're a red head, a Sagittarius, or the oldest child. We often confuse valid reasons and lame excuses.

On the other hand, if I overemphasize Adjustment I'm at risk of trying to become someone else and never feeling good enough, never feeling I measure up. The goal of self-improvement becomes a futile and defeating pursuit of perfection. It becomes a form of planting self-acceptance on the distant horizon, a place I can never reach. Any literal horizon is actually a visual illusion. If you walk towards the horizon, it just moves, right? Perfection is an elusive horizon where there are no residents or even visitors.

Therefore, the healthy stance is to seek to understand and accept yourself, and with that greater knowledge of yourself, seek to grow as a person to be the best version of you—for yourself and for those you're in relationship with. And the healthy stance continually engages that creative tension between acceptance and adjustment. Furthermore, the understanding of your personality will be most beneficial and transforming when you engage that creative tension between Acceptance and Adjustment.

For example, I do well to accept and even embrace that I'm an Enneagram 2. I can see a consistency of my personality being expressed across many different types of environments and situations, and I can see its pattern in my life throughout my history. It's okay to say to myself, "This is who I am."

Along with accepting my core personality style as a 2, I need to be willing to make adjustments that enable me to be the healthiest version of myself and my personality.

I believe that growth in any area of my life (personally, vocationally, relationally, spiritually, physically, etc.) lies just outside my comfort zone. If I just stay within my current comfort zone, there's little or no growth. If I go too far outside my comfort zone, I'm likely to strive for something I cannot reach or may reach briefly but cannot sustain.

This is why unusual or extreme diets and exercise routines don't work—you're either defeated before you even get started or you follow the diet or fitness program for a while but quit because it's not sustainable. It's too much of a change to become a part of your lifestyle.

When we are seeking to change anything, especially ourselves, we do well to hit the sweet spot where Meaningful and Manageable overlap. There are many goals I could set that would be very meaningful but are not manageable because they're not realistic and achievable. I could set a goal for myself to lose 20 pounds in the month of December, and if accomplished, that would be very meaningful and beneficial for me. But losing 20 pounds in 31 days isn't happening, at least not for me...unless I amputate my left leg after Christmas or I do a 30-day juice cleanse, and I'll pass on both methods.

Okay, what about losing just one pound in December? Well, that's a very manageable goal. Dropping a single pound of weight in four weeks is quite realistic and doable. But it's not very meaningful, is it? The loss of a single pound is not going to make much of a difference in my health or my waistline.

Okay, what if I set a goal of losing 1 pound per week? Now, that's getting closer to meeting the criteria for a December goal and achievement that is both meaningful and manageable. I'm giving myself a realistic chance to achieve something important and valuable to me. Plus, there's a better chance I'll repeat the goal and effort in January.

Dropping 8 pounds in two months is doable with meaningful outcomes—look better and feel better, plus the invisible benefits of better heart health. And 4 pounds a month is almost 50 pounds at the end of a year, which would make a profound difference. Heck, even 2 pounds a month would give you almost 25 pounds at year's end, and that's a weight reduction you would definitely see and feel.

Setting meaningful and manageable goals and making meaningful and manageable changes over time makes significant positive differences, and as a bonus it builds our confidence and boosts our self-esteem.

Let's bring this back to Enneagram work with the reminder that you do not need to change your core personality. Besides, you couldn't if you tried. If you're a 4, accept and embrace your 4ness. And make some meaningful and manageable adjustments to become the healthiest 4 you can be. If you're an 8, fantastic. The world needs healthy 8s. So, the question for you becomes, "How can I make a few positive and reasonable changes to be the healthiest 8 I can be, both for myself and for those I'm in relationship with?"

2

THE ENNEAGRAM IN YOUR CLOSEST RELATIONSHIP

―――――――

"Your understanding of who you are affects every relationship you enter into and try to maintain."
  –Suzanne Stabile

Personality in Couples Work

For many years I've lamented that there is a gap in the models developed and taught by the couples therapy researchers and practitioners I highly respect and follow. That gap is the understanding of the impact of each partner's unique personality. The closest thing I've seen in our field of couples therapy to acknowledging the influence of core individual factors are the following:

1. Attachment Theory and the three attachment styles

2. Differences between men and women

3. A partner with past and/or present trauma

4. A partner with a current addiction

5. A partner with a significant mental health issue

Those five factors are absolutely valid. However, note that of those five factors, the last three represent a big problem or at least a significant complication one partner is bringing into the relationship dynamic.

Within the first factor of Attachment Theory and its three styles of relational attachment, only one of the styles is truly healthy.

Regarding the second factor, theorists, therapists, and authors have offered an understanding of the differences between men and women—mainly how the two genders in a relationship think differently, communicate differently, and have differing core needs and desires. Books like "Men Are from Mars, Women Are from Venus" and those that followed explored some of the core differences of the two sexes.

However, even the helpful study of gender differences, in its logical limits, pulls up short by only being able to examine neutral or positive differences in two broad categories—men and women. But every man or woman is also a unique individual with a distinct personality.

My concern is that the field of couples therapy often seems to either not know how to factor in non-negative elements of individual personality OR the field of study and practice doesn't consider it important. Regardless of the reasons, I believe that this neglect creates a gap in couples therapy and misses an opportunity in relationship enrichment.

Blind Spots

As a couples therapist, an additional reason I'm an advocate of each partner knowing their personality type, is that thoughtfully doing so presses both individuals to consider their own tendencies and weaknesses rather than just complaining about their partner's habits and shortcomings.

Not only are most of us reluctant to critique our own relationship behaviors and confess our own faults, we also have blind spots. My current automobile has a significant blind spot behind my left shoulder when I'm driving. I'm not ignoring the SUV coming up on my left; it's actually invisible to me for a second. Because of the blind spot I must be extra careful when I'm changing lanes and merging left. And I don't assume someone will make space for me just because they see my turn signal.

Likewise, our personal and relational blind spots are not attitudes and behaviors we are in denial about; rather they are tendencies we genuinely can't see. But we need to know about our blind spots, whether in a car or in a relationship, because without awareness and attentiveness to them we will collide with others and do damage.

Author Jeff Goins says, "Ignorance is not bliss. What you don't know and don't understand as a weakness has the capacity to control you. What you do know and understand gives you the capacity to have more control over the weakness."

Says Ian Morgan Cron, the point of personality work is "self-understanding and growing beyond the self-defeating dimensions of our personality, as well as improving relationships and growing in compassion for others."

I believe that one of the keys to unwrapping this riddle that is me, this riddle wrapped in mystery inside an enigma, is to do this personal exploration and work. But do not mistake greater self-understanding as an egocentric project and mere psychological navel-gazing. We are never an island unto ourselves, so the great goal and benefit of such self-understanding and personal growth is improved relationships.

In the previous chapter I mentioned two things about the Enneagram that have such significant implications for your closest relationships that I'm going to briefly repeat them here.

Understanding to the 4th Power

Earlier I wrote that my wife, Dorrie, and I discovered that when both of us understood our own Enneagram personality type as well as each other's primary type the level of helpful insight for our relationship was multiplied by four! We came to refer to it as "Insight to the 4th power."

Do you see how impactful that could be in a relationship if both partners had a fuller understanding of themselves and their partner?

To illustrate how profound and potentially transformative that can be, consider that when you seek to repair a leaky faucet or fix a lawn mower that won't start, you can rely on a single level of insight and understanding. You just need to know enough about the parts and their function to make the repairs.

You don't need insights about yourself to fix the faucet. The mower has no insights about itself or about you to help you along. It's simply up to you to know how to repair or replace the key parts. That's single directional understanding, which is sufficient for being a handy man, but single directional understanding is woefully inadequate for being a husband.

And how single directional understanding works in a relationship is that it makes the (false) assumption that I know what makes you tick, what your problem is, so therefore I know how to fix you.

This is one of the reasons I have such a negative reaction when I hear a wife say to me, "I know my husband better than he knows himself." (And I hear husbands say it about their wives.) It's such an absurd statement! How can I possibly know anyone better than they know themselves when I am a mystery to myself? I've been with me every single day for six decades now and I'm still making pleasant (and unpleasant) discoveries about myself.

Yes, as I said above in this chapter, we all have blind spots. But don't mistake a person's blind spot for you having expert knowledge they don't have, which borders on implying that you have the psychic powers of mindreading and fortunetelling plus multiple advanced degrees in psychology along with X-ray vision.

So, to summarize this point, unilateral understanding of another person is not only limited; it is presumptuous at best. Now, a singular and better understanding of myself is a wise and beneficial objective, and it is the right place to start. Let me repeat this for emphasis. Seek to understand more about yourself first.

But don't limit yourself to self-understanding. Also seek to genuinely understand your partner for even further benefit. I'll tell you as a therapist that it's a powerful thing for a person to feel understood. Not heard and diagnosed but listened to and understood. And you don't have to be a trained therapist to enable someone to experience that good feeling.

Lastly, may you and your partner seek and benefit from Insight to the 4th Power. May you and your significant other both seek to more deeply understand yourselves and each other.

Acceptance and Adjustment

I also made this point earlier, but it bears repeating here because of the 4-way implications if practiced by both partners in a relationship. I wrote that I'm convinced that the Enneagram is an excellent tool for increasing self-understanding, and with that greater self-understanding a person can then engage what I refer to as the "creation tension between Acceptance and Adjustment."

In a previous chapter I emphasized the importance of pairing Acceptance with Adjustment. Furthermore, I maintained that Adjustments should be Meaningful but also Manageable. These two creative tensions between Acceptance & Adjustment and Meaningful & Manageable very much come into play in the relationship with our significant other.

Specifically, is the adjustment I'm making or being asked to make meaningful enough for my partner and manageable enough for me?

Picture Meaningful and Manageable on a set of scales or on a seesaw. What would be very desirable and meaningful to Sandy might feel unreasonable or unmanageable to Alex. On the other hand, an adjustment that feels very realistic to Alex might not be enough of a tweak to make a difference to Sandy.

Here's an example of acceptance and adjustment working together. Alex has a quick wit and a delightful sense of humor. He has enjoyed humor and comedy and making people laugh since he was in middle school. He's a walking unpaid stand-up comic. His humor is usually appropriate and enjoyable. Alex is just plain fun to have around.

Sometimes, however, Alex can try to lighten the mood in the room when it's not really appropriate. Sometimes Alex will use humor to diffuse the tension with Sandy or to avoid conflict with her. Sandy once said to Alex, "Sometimes it feels like I'm trying to have a serious conversation with Robin Williams while he's in character on stage."

If Sandy were to request Alex to cease being a comedian and generally become a serious person at all times, that would not only violate accepting a core part of who Alex is, it would be setting Alex up for failure and setting Sandy up for frustration.

However, if Sandy accepts and affirms Alex for his sense of humor, she is being completely reasonable when requesting Alex to dial back his comedy routine at the reception following a funeral they're attending. Also, her request that Alex take their occasional difficult conversations more seriously in the moment is a reasonable request as well.

If Alex's defensive response to Sally's request for those minor situational adjustments is, "You're trying to change me. You're not accepting me for who I am," then Alex is the one being unreasonable by his refusal to make small manageable adjustments which still leave enormous room for him to be his humorous self. In essence, Sally is asking for a 2 percent shift and Alex reacts as if it were a demand for a complete overhaul.

Putting It Together and What If

Think with me for just a moment. What if you and your partner each invested yourselves in gaining Insight to the 4th Power AND each of you engaged the creative tension between Acceptance and Adjustment, and within Adjustment you each navigated the sweet spot between Meaningful and Manageable. Can you see how profoundly that could transform each of you individually and also your relationship?

If you can only hold a glimpse of that possibility right now, that's okay. Stay with us and keep reading. We're confident that as an exploration of the Enneagram and an understanding of your own personality begins to take shape and make sense, you will have many "aha" moments and will see the encouraging possibilities for your relationship.

Part II

Identifying Your Position on the Field

3

TYPE 1: THE SELF-CRITICIZING REFORMER

Main Desire: To be "good" and honorable

Main Fear: Being "bad" or imperfect in some way

Go-To Hang-Up: Allowing your inner critic/shadow self/dark passenger to guide your thoughts

Path to Personal Growth: Accept your past mistakes and learn from them, acknowledging that there is often more than one "right" way. Realize you don't negatively affect others as much as you give yourself credit for. Learn to swap "perfection" for "work in progress." Choose to see yourself as a good person.

I have never seen myself as a perfectionist. Isn't it common knowledge that "nobody's perfect" and that perfectionism does not and cannot actually exist?

Yet still, my wife of 15 years has revealed to me that I indeed have a perfectionist tendency. I have also repeatedly been told by people who have worked alongside me, "You are a very detailed person."

Apparently, I continue to prove I am a perfectionist by rebelling against the very idea: I carry shame regarding how truly imperfect I am. Therefore, I subconsciously apply pressure on myself to *not be* a "bad person".

As I am now in my 40s, I often struggle when I am reunited with any of my former classmates. I have to refrain from saying, "I remember back in 3rd grade, we were playing dodgeball in gym class. I caught the ball you threw, causing you to get out. As soon as I did, I think I made a face that basically said, "Sorry 'bout your luck!' I just want to let you know I've changed. I've grown up. I've matured. I'm a much more empathetic person now. Please forgive me for how I was prideful that day back in 1990. I really am sorry."

Now, if I said that out loud to them, I am confident their immediate response would be, "What are you talking about? How can you even remember something like that from so long ago?"

The Enneagram 1 in me means I keep beating myself up over all the stupid stuff I did and said that most people have no memory of, yet I still carry with me. I didn't forget, even if they did. I still have one foot in the doorway. They clearly moved on, but I guess I stayed.

It's like I feel the need to go on an apology tour to make things right from my former life. I want to tell each individual person that I am sorry. Better late than never.

Only, what if the only evidence of my perceived crime is locked away in my mind? Perhaps a tree has fallen in the forest and I'm the only one who heard it. Would it make me a better person if I convinced everyone I'd learned my lesson? Would they be able to see I'm a different me than the one who lived in less humility?

So yeah, that's a glimpse at the Enneagram 1 in me. That's my inner critic, my shadow self, my dark passenger.

I see it as a crucial exercise, for every man, to make a Top 5 list of the men who have most profoundly influenced his life. By recognizing who these men are, we can begin to assess and accept that to some degree, we are who we are, at least in part because who they are/were to us. And a significant part of their impact upon us is connected to how those men expressed their Enneagram personality type in their lives...and into our lives.

Undeniably, one of the most influential men in my own life was born in Kenosha, Wisconsin, on March 29th, 1930. His given name was Alberto Victorio Metallo.

I simply knew him as Papaw; which was quite ironic, because despite the obviously Southern name I called him, he is probably the main reason I don't actually have an Alabama accent, which is the state I was born and raised in.

By the time I was born in 1981, Papaw had already been living in the South for nearly a decade. He only lived a few miles down the road from me, so I pretty much saw him on a weekly basis.

I wouldn't fully realize it until I was an adult, but this first-generation Italian American man from the Midwest would ultimately write much of my personal coding for what I perceived it meant to be a man.

It would just so happen that what I saw as some of Papaw's quirks were actually signs of him being an Enneagram 1. With that being said, Enneagram 1 is hardwired into my concept of manliness.

Both my sister and my mom have made a point to tell me how much I remind them of him. So even though I am not an Enneagram 1, I personally know what it's like to see the world through that filter.

Here are some of the giveaway hints that Papaw was a shareable example of what Enneagram 1, The Self-Criticizing Reformer, looks like in a man:

He lived in a small ranch style home on five acres and spent much of his weekend meticulously mowing his lawn in a certain perfect pattern that was so particular he had to do it himself.

I can't think of a time when I walked into his house that there was ever a sign of clutter. In fact, every time I remember going to his house, during the middle of the visit, he would pull out his vacuum and clean the living room floor... while everyone else there was still in the room.

But when I think of a person who is an Enneagram 1, it's more than just someone who is a perfectionist; it is also a person who is inclined to reform others.

Growing up in my own house, when certain young gentlemen would come to visit unannounced, in an attempt to convert us to their religion, my mom would make a big dramatic scene: *"Hurry! Close the shades! Turn off all the lights! Be quiet! Don't let them hear you so they will think no one is home!"*

Let's just say that was the complete opposite of how Papaw would handle the situation. He openly invited all door-to-door evangelists into his home.

It was never a short visit. He truly loved spending hours

debating with them, in an attempt to convert them instead of giving them a chance to try to convert him.

But despite his strict principles, I saw him as one of the most fun adults I knew as a kid. He would regularly invite me and my sister over to spend the night at his house.

It was always a mystery to me, but for some reason, he always had these huge empty barrels behind his shop.

At the top of the biggest hill in his yard, Papaw would hold the two barrels in place, as my sister and I each crawled into one, and then he would push us both at the same time to see who would win the race down to the bottom of the hill.

After each race, we would push our empty barrels back up the hill for him to do it again. We did it enough times that neither of us could stop laughing from all the excitement, nor walk in a straight line due to the dizziness.

This event would always end with the hilarious finale, where Papaw would crouch down into one of the barrels himself and have me and my sister push him down the hill enough times until he was as silly and dizzy as we were.

At their best, in their growth state, Enneagram 1s will act more like an Enneagram 7. I think this story perfectly demonstrates that.

So now that I have illustrated how my grandfather was an Enneagram 1, it's time to take a look at how I have it in me as well, since after all, we all are a bit of all nine types.

I have an extremely close relationship with Enneagram 1- as it is one of my wings. (See page 149–151 about Wings.) Enneagram 1 provides a strong framework for stability and consistency, but it's also a place where I find myself in times of *prolonged crisis*.

It's the all-or-nothing mentality of Enneagram 1 that I morph into when I am in true survivor mode.

The funny thing is, in hindsight, I realize now that I most likely spent the slight majority of my 30s looking, thinking, and acting like an Enneagram 1 because I was indeed in survival mode.

When my wife and I were both 29, we had our first child. We decided to take a leap of faith, moving away from our secure jobs in Nashville to my hometown in Alabama... without jobs lined up. And this was long before the post-Covid "work from home" era we now live in.

I know. You're right. We should have known better.

So of course, we lasted about nine months there until our savings at the time ran out and we had to ask for our old jobs back in Tennessee.

At the exact halfway point on the move back, my wife's car broke down on the highway and we had to buy a new one, though we had just ran through our savings.

For the next several years, I apparently was "starving" for some sense of control over my own life. This is the time of my life when my Enneagram 1 wing/alter-ego kicked into gear.

I became a vegan. *The bad kind of vegan.* The kind that made my lifestyle everyone else's problem and I openly judged others for not making the "right" choice that I was making.

As much as I feel ashamed now when I think about those years, I also believe that the arbitrary construct of living by such strict guidelines not only gave me that sense of control over my life that I needed, but it also provided a distraction to allow enough time to pass for everything to rebuild.

Eventually, I changed employers; and when I did, my salary doubled. By then my wife and I had saved up enough money to buy the last affordable new house in one of the nicest school zones in the state to raise not only our son, but eventually our new daughter as well.

I had finally earned the life experience points to give me the confidence (and financial security) I needed to feel in control of my life. Sure enough, soon after, I suddenly one day stopped being vegan.

Granted, I transitioned to being a vegetarian, and eventually to where I am now- a much more balanced approach of being reasonable about my calories during the week based on protein, fat, and fiber, and then having a little bit more fun on the weekends.

Throughout our marriage, my wife has made a habit of reminding me of one of her life mottos, "Everything in moderation."

Hearing that had historically been difficult for me. However, she's right. So much of my own personal growth over the years has been when I found a happy medium between two extremes.

One of the biggest revelations I've discovered about myself since diving deep into the world of the Enneagram, is the concept of the shadow self.

Here's what I learned: I have always made it part of my identity to be very kind, warm, and accepting to everyone around me. Well, everyone, that is, except for one person.

That's right- *me*. It was like I somehow deserved less than what I was giving to the world around me.

I have since released myself from the captivity of that mindset. My shadow self (a harsh critic whose job was to provide structure and stability) has been reformed and redeemed.

I feel a sense of inner peace now that I haven't felt in a very long time.

So now, I am turning the mirror to you: Do you see these traits in yourself? Is there an inner critic who speaks to you on a daily basis, telling you that it has to be black or white, all or nothing?

This concept was first revealed to me a few years ago when I read the book, *The Four Agreements*. Wrote author Ruiz, "In your whole life, no one has abused you more than you have abused yourself. And your limit of self-abuse is exactly the limit you will tolerate from someone else. If someone abuses you more than you abuse yourself, you will probably walk away from that person."

Imagine how would you feel if you heard that judgmental narrator in your own head speak to others the way you allow it to speak to yourself?

You'd be angry. You would do whatever you needed to do to prevent that voice from hurting anyone around you. Because you are a person who is wired to do what is right, that includes standing up for those who are being taken advantage of and who need to be empowered.

It's quite the confusing paradox to realize for the first time in your life that you are angry at yourself for being so hard on yourself, while also recognizing that the original intent was for that inner critic to serve as a guide to protect you.

Imagine the necessity of a nation building its military to be strong enough to protect its own people. Now imagine if that military becomes so effective and efficient, it actually becomes overpowering to its own people, and it eventually attempts to police the rest of the world in the name of protection.

I believe that men who are Enneagram 1s, or at least those of us with those tendencies, know exactly what it's like to feed the beast to the point the beast begins to hurt us instead of helping us.

In her book *Enneagram Empowerment*, author Laura Miltenberger explains it like this: "Your Enneagram number doesn't only show you your patterns of behavior that are holding you back, it also shows you the pain that drives that behavior. It's important to look at this pain with warmth and self-compassion, so that you can find freedom from the pain that is trapping you into those loops of unhelpful behavior."

The next challenge becomes verbalizing this habit in yourself, as most men I know were continually taught throughout their lives to "man up."

And we know what "man up" means: Deny your feelings and emotions, bury them down deep and whatever you do... don't talk about them, because that will make you look weak, and people won't respect you.

As Dr. Phil likes to say, "How's that working for you?"

The answer? It causes men to be resentful, angry, anxious, depressed, and confused.

Enneagram 1s already struggle with an "all or nothing" mindset. The balanced solution is to share with the people who are most involved in your life, such as your wife, immediate family and closest friends, what you are learning about yourself.

I'll admit, it is a possibility that not everyone you confide in will understand fully what you are going through. But if they are truly someone you value, and they value you, then they will likely appreciate you nurturing that relationship by being vulnerable.

The reality is that most people you confide in will likely respond with something like this: "Well, I could've told you that. You are way too hard on yourself."

What it reminds me of is when you see a video clip of yourself and think, "Is that really the way I sound? Is that really the way I look? Is that really the way I act?"

When we begin to understand what's really going on deep on the inside, we ironically get a better look at how people already perceive us from the outside.

The part they are not aware of is exactly how critical we are on the inside. By admitting we have an inner critic, it creates a concept of accountability to ourselves and others.

Consider this: I am in my early 40s and just now understanding this is how I've been operating for the past few decades. That's a lot of unpacking and sorting out to do.

Chances are, you've got at least as much deconstruction and then reconstruction to do as I do.

I have to remind myself throughout the day not to let the captor take over.

I have to remind myself not to give myself such a hard time, but instead, to extend the same level of grace and understanding that I would to anyone else on the problem.

That can be difficult to get started when you're so accustomed to giving yourself no grace and understanding.

Can you relate to the struggles of the Self-Criticizing Reformer?

If so, I have good news for you. You are specifically designed for this task: To perfectly reform yourself.

Imagine watching a movie where after nearly two hours of the villain being evil, in the final scene they have a change of heart and decide to be good now instead.

That sudden and drastic transformation is not the norm, though there are some notable exceptions: *The Grinch*, Gru in

Despicable Me, and Darth Vader in *Return of the Jedi*. (Sorry for just spoiling a Star Wars movie that is now over 40 years old!)

Your shadow self has a backstory and needs to find redemption; like the Grinch, Gru, and Darth Vader. Your shadow self did what he thought he had to do out of self-preservation, perhaps never slowing down that cadence even though a recalibration was long overdue.

The Enneagram 1 in you means that the hero inside of you helps heal the villain inside of you.

It is time for your shadow self to be reformed and redeemed.

4

TYPE 2: THE SELF-DENYING HIDDEN WARRIOR

Main Desire: To be wanted and perceived as irreplaceable

Main Fear: To not be needed and appreciated

Go-To Hang-Up: Focusing on serving others and fulfilling their needs, neglecting your own needs

Path to Personal Growth: Accept that you have needs and acknowledge that you are valuable aside from people needing you. Realize the importance of others making you happy by helping you, recognizing that you can still love people even though you can't "save" them all. Choose to see yourself as being loved by others with no strings attached.

Ramon here. Nick has invited to comment on my being a Two:

I've taken numerous Enneagram assessments, and my two highest scores are consistent in suggesting that I'm a 2, followed so closely by a 9 that it's drafting on the 2's bumper and trying to pass. I like to say I'm a 2 with a 9 riding on my back.

That I'm a counselor is no surprise to anyone who currently knows me or anyone who knew me as a child. I like to help people. Growing up as an only child in a single parent household, I was helpful to my mother. As a 6-year-old, I had responsibilities inside the house and in the yard that my friends and peers didn't have. I don't recall thinking it unfair and resenting it; it's just how it was when there was a house to run and take care of, and there was just the two of us. My mother worked full-time (even more during tax season) and never remarried. It was just logical that she needed my help.

Growing up as an only child of a single mom also shaped me in another way that factors into my 2ness. By nature, only children tend to be self-sufficient and independent. Have that child be raised for the next 12 years by an independent and self-sufficient mother and you'll get an adult who is unaccustomed to asking for help and is uncomfortable receiving it.

The combination means that I'm in my comfort zone being a helper and outside of my comfort zone when I'm receiving help.

When someone does something kind and unexpected for me, I'm not only appreciative, I become effusive in my expression of gratitude. The running joke in our family is that I'm an "over-thanker." You should see to what extent I go to thank another driver in traffic for letting me merge in front of them. I respond with more waves and hand signals than a 3rd base coach veiling his bunt sign to a batter at the plate. I stop just short of asking for the gracious driver's address so I can send a handwritten thank-you note.

But here's the dark side of that scenario for a Two. If I allow someone to merge in front of me (which I do a LOT because that is what a Two does) I expect a Thank-You wave. And not just a slight head nod or half-hearted pinky finger lift from the steering wheel. I want a wave that says, "Thank you, kind sir. This world would certainly be a better place if there were more people like you in it." And I always respond to an adequate "thank you" wave with a visible "you're welcome" wave.

When I let someone merge in front of me, or I pause and give someone room to let them turn left, while I hold back traffic behind me like Moses held back the Red Sea, I expect a "thank you" wave. And if I don't get the wave, I'm not a happy Camry camper.

"Does that driver think I'm obligated to let him in front of me? Does he believe a wave isn't warranted? I wonder what other things in life this narcissist arrogantly feels entitled to. Oh look, he has one of those yellow "Don't Tread on Me" license plates. Big surprise. Yes, it's all about you, fella. We're all here for you. I feel sorry for your wife, if you still have one. Thanks to guys like you I will always have job security as a marriage therapist." (Twos often have an active monologue running in their heads.)

As a Two, I genuinely find helping others meaningful and fulfilling, and I don't serve others in order to be thanked and praised. And yet, feeling taken for granted makes my X-Men Wolverine claws begin to come out, as does feeling used or being manipulated by someone I'm helping.

I hide a subtle insecurity, even from myself—a belief that my value in a relationship, my likeability, my being loved and loveable, is not just enhanced by being a helper, it may be dependent on it. If I'm not a thoughtful and generous encourager, what do I have to offer someone in a friendship?

One of the ways a 2 can encourage others is to help them lighten their burden a bit with laughter. I enjoy making people laugh. I've been a class clown since elementary school. I'd do things like walk up to the pencil sharpener on the wall and dramatically act like I was fighting to reel in a giant fish. My classmates would laugh, and my teacher would chide me back to my seat. People like people who entertain them and make them laugh. They're fun to have around. And I like people to like me. I want people to like me. As a 2, more than I want people to be impressed by me or admire me, I want them to like me. And that means that I can slip into being a people pleaser. And this is when my 9ness slips in a side door and takes the stage. I'll address my 9ness in that chapter.

Now, here's Nick again...

You have to be from Alabama like I was to know this, but it is custom anytime a new baby is born in my home state that a self-appointed family member decides for you whether you will be a lifelong "Roll Tide" fan or a "War Eagle" fan.

My Uncle Al was that person for me. For the record, he dubbed me as a "Roll Tide" fan, representing the University of Alabama.

So early in this book, I am going to make a revelation about myself that quite ironically will cause me to "get my man card pulled"... but here it is:

I don't even know how to play football– nor have I, nor will I, ever have a desire to learn how it works.

However, my ignorance of the rules of football is irrelevant.

Anytime a person learns I am originally from Alabama, and they ask me which team I root for, I know how to answer, without hesitation.

My Uncle Al not only served as a helper by choosing my favorite football team for me, but he also always ensured that my sister and I had plenty of presents to open on Christmas morning (in addition to what my parents got for us). And the tradition seamlessly continued once I had my own kids.

But even more than the gifts at Christmas, anytime there was ever any kind of family gathering, he was there. He showed up for every holiday, every graduation, and every play.

His faithful physical presence helped provide a sense of belonging and worthiness I have always been wired to need. In that regard, he was giving me a gift that he didn't even realize the perceived value of.

When I was in 6th grade, Uncle Al decided to pick me up and drive me an hour away to go to the nearest mall on one random, otherwise boring summer day.

It was then that I was first introduced to the most amazing restaurant I had never heard of until that point in my life: Applebee's. That was over 30 years ago, but I still remember what I ordered . . .The Clubhouse Grille.

I never took Uncle Al for granted in how he kept continually showing up in my life, but if there was a person I could take for granted throughout my life, it would have been him.

That's how I know he's an Enneagram 2. My Uncle Al is a giver.

When I first started learning about the Enneagram, I assumed there must surely be a shortage of Enneagram 2 males in the world. Clearly, the "most masculine Enneagram" had to be the

Enneagram 8, who represents strength and power, like pretty much every WWE wrestler ever.

It was challenging for me to understand the concept of a male who is driven by a fundamental desire to help others, as opposed to a desire to be seen as successful like an Enneagram 3, or self-sufficient like an Enneagram 5, or dependable like an Enneagram 6, or a negotiator like an Enneagram 9...

At the initial glance, none of the adjectives I heard to describe 2s seemed to click with the immediate stereotypes of men that I had in my mind: *empathetic, warm-hearted, and caring.*

But once I allowed myself to be more open-minded, I was eventually able to see how other descriptive words for an Enneagram 2 definitely described identifiable concepts of masculinity: *Self-sacrificing, generous, hidden warrior.*

The funny thing is, I happen to know plenty of male 2s, and have throughout my entire life– much more so than the number of male 8s that are in my social circle.

Chances are, you too are surrounded by men who are Enneagram 2s, though their traditional male identity and interests are causing their true self to be less obvious, hidden somewhere beneath all the testosterone.

So, while I have curated a collection of stereotypes of what each of the nine Enneagram personalities looks like on a male, to help me establish a quick baseline when I am working to determine which Enneagram type a man is, I know the reality is that a person's Enneagram profile is more like a map.

If I can figure out which of the 9 possible maps that a person is fundamentally using to navigate their world, it can help me understand what is really going on inside of them, despite how they perceive themselves or how others perceive them.

I personally share a common trait with Enneagram 2s, as Enneagram 9s also tend to be people-pleasers. We see this with my favorite character from *The Office*, who I perceive to be a male Enneagram 2: Andy Bernard.

In the episode "The Merger," where Andy sets his goal to become the Number 2 man in Scranton by "name repetition, personality mirroring, and never breaking off a handshake," he demonstrates his main desire of wanting to be wanted and perceived as irreplaceable, and he shows his fear of being undesirable; so much so, that his strategy is to forsake his own identify in the process.

Not to mention, his ultimate objective is not to become the Number 1 man, but instead, the Number 2 man. He simply wants to become the "helper" of the person actually in charge.

A season later in the episode "The Return," Andy smothers his boss, Michael, which leads to him saying the classic line, "Sorry I annoyed you with my friendship!" This is an example of how an Enneagram 2 can become needy in relationships, especially when they are under pressure.

The self-preservation instinct (see pages 154-160 about Instincts) of the Enneagram 2 will, at times, resemble a child trying to get their needs met without asking. A perfect example is in the cringiest episode ever of *The Office*, "Scott's Tots," where Michael Scott has to address the fact that Andy's habit of "talking baby talk" has become obnoxious to his coworkers.

And of course, perhaps one of the most obvious indications that Andy is an Enneagram 2 is when we see him in the aforementioned episode "The Return" where in an act of rage, he punches through a wall, in response to Jim's prank of hiding Andy's cell phone above the ceiling panel.

Though Enneagram 2s are typically seen as accommodating, they tap into their inner Enneagram 8 when they find themselves in stress, which is the complete opposite of who they normally are.

Following this same logic, it would not be a stretch to label Ross Gellar from *Friends* as an Enneagram 2. He is consistently portrayed as the most sensitive of the group.

He has a tendency to be childlike: Ross proudly dresses up in costume as the Holiday Armadillo to try to relate to his son. It is later revealed that Ross never stopped visiting his childhood pediatrician and still gets excited to choose a lollipop at the end of each visit.

Despite his overall gentle demeanor, Ross will instantly transform into his Enneagram 8 stress mode: *"We were on a break!"*

Recently, my wife hesitantly mentioned to me, "Sometimes I wonder if you are a 2. You do so much for other people, but I wonder if that's your way of feeling loved?"

That was a statement I immediately interpreted as a compliment; especially because I will be the first person to tell you that I am not nice enough to be an Enneagram 2!

The thing is, if there were hidden cameras in my house, or if you spotted me out with my family, it wouldn't be outlandish to assume that I am a people-pleasing Enneagram 2.

An Enneagram 2 is a person who subconsciously aims to make themselves irreplaceable and wanted by serving others.

When I am in dad mode, as well as husband mode, I am constantly focused on the next way I can serve my family. I take care of all the garbage and recycling, I clean all the bathrooms, I take care of any plumbing issues, I constantly clean any dishes in the kitchen sink, I take most of the photos of our family, I am the initiator of conversations at the dinner table, I coordinate family game nights, and I am the emotional counselor for our family.

I definitely feel like an Enneagram 2 when my kids insist on my wife doing something for them, like making popcorn for example, despite me clearly announcing, "I'm available. I will do it right now."

This is of course met in response to either of my kids declaring, "No, I want Mommy to do it." Looking back, throughout my entire life, I have been wired to help people, and when my help is rejected, it has made me feel personally rejected, to some degree.

If much of my identity is to help people, and they reject my offer to help them, it is not always easy for me to accept. It's something I personally am working through.

Another way I can falsely appear as a 2 is that being a mentor is one of my favorite hobbies. I have always loved serving as a guide and coach to other people. Whether it was the Peer Helpers Club when I was in high school to help underclassmen, or when I volunteered two summers in college to be an elementary school teacher in Thailand, or when I volunteered to mentor an at-risk teenage boy for a couple of years, teaching him to play chess as a way for us to bond.

Even at the Publix grocery store near my house, where I do most of my family's grocery shopping (another way to serve my family), I ultimately serve as a mentor to several of the young workers there who are working their way through college, as I offer them direction about their uncertain future in planning their careers.

"I know what it's like being 20 years old and not knowing what you're supposed to be when you grow up... I didn't even know what my actual major was until later on in college," I have explained to all of my unofficial mentorship attendees as they ring up my groceries.

A couple of years ago while on vacation with my family in Destin, Florida, my kids wanted to visit the local Walmart to look at their stuffed animals for their allotted "souvenir budget."

As we made our way through the ocean of a parking lot to get to the store entrance, I spotted a family consisting of a single mom and her four kids. The oldest son was attempting to remove a flat tire on their SUV while holding his phone watching a YouTube tutorial.

I immediately abandoned "Operation Stuffed Animal Souvenirs" and ran towards the family with the flat tire.

The highlight of that trip to Florida with my family was being able to teach that teenage boy how to properly change a flat tire. My job wasn't done until I showed him and his mother the best lug wrench and hydraulic jack to purchase, inside the Walmart, to better prepare for the next time they ended up with a flat tire.

As I continue explaining my perceived likeness of an Enneagram 2, we can't forget the fact that I am a rare demographic:

Not that many dudes are into the Enneagram. My ultimate motive in getting certified in the Enneagram was not actually to understand myself better. Instead, it was because I wanted to understand others better and help them to be the best version of themselves.

However, I know I would have to practice on myself first, if I could ever begin to help others with the knowledge of the Enneagram.

Helping people is, and always has been, one of my favorite things to do... for fun!

You may be thinking right now: "Are you sure you're not a 2?

It really sounds like you're describing how a male Enneagram 2 would think and act!"

As much as I would love to identify as "selfless," my motives in doing so would simply be "selfish," and if you're looking for a classic case of irony, that would be it.

I'm too aware of the importance of maintaining boundaries with other people. That's the most obvious giveaway that I'm not a 2. I'm way too suspicious of people to give them a chance to walk over me.

True 2s have a lifelong struggle of not knowing, often until it's too late, that they have been taken advantage of, in their desire to help others.

Another way I know I'm not an Enneagram 2 is because they have this habit of focusing on helping others, but not themselves.

Even though I would definitely put "helping others" in my *Top 5 Hobbies* list, my Enneagram 1 wing is too strong to prevent me from going easy on myself.

It goes back to that safety training speech I always ignore on planes, where the flight attendants remind you to put on your own oxygen mask before trying to help others.

Let that serve as a symbol of what it's like for an Enneagram 2 male throughout his life: He will try to help everyone else put on their oxygen masks before he puts on his own, which might potentially prevent him from helping as many people in the long run.

Whereas it can be natural for an Enneagram 1 to serve as their harshest critic, an Enneagram 2 has the tendency instead to completely forsake being hard on himself, and instead redirect this energy into finding value in feeling needed by others.

Can you relate to the struggles of the Self-Denying Hidden Warrior?

If so, I have good news for you. You are specifically designed for this task: To help other people, as well as yourself.

In a culture where acting tough is synonymous with the male identity, the truth is, the world is full of male 2s out there who are perhaps covertly doing their job despite us knowing it.

I could easily imagine how most male 2s never get the credit for their true Enneagram identity.

Think of a man you know who serves in the military, or coaches a sports team, or is a paramedic or car mechanic or a truck driver. It is quite possible he is an Enneagram 2, thus partially explaining the reason he is so drawn to and skilled at serving his country, his team, or his local community.

I think there's a good chance we are taking our male Enneagram 2s for granted; not only because 2s are the most selfless and most likely to serve others, and therefore, have the biggest struggle with laying down personal boundaries and focusing on self-care.

We also take them for granted because that servant's heart might be overshadowed by his tattoo sleeves, his pick-up truck, or his hunting gear.

It should not be a surprise that the most famous and legendary superhero is an Enneagram 2. The Man of Steel, himself. Yes, Superman is a 2.

I hereby invite you to secretly ponder every man you care about in your life. Try to see them through the lens of an Enneagram 2. Could they actually be the least obvious Enneagram for a male, which prevents their actual identity from being known?

If you can't name at least three male 2s in your social circle, I would suggest it's a sign you haven't yet figured out who those Self-Denying Hidden Warriors are.

5

TYPE 3: THE SELF-SHAMING ACHIEVER

———————

Main Desire: To be successful and important

Main Fear: Losing, feeling worthless

Go-To Hang-Up: Feeling the need to "win" at everything, while secretly feeling like an imposter

Path to Personal Growth: Accept that you have flaws (like the rest of us) and that is okay. Acknowledge that it is important to let your guard down with people who know you best, realizing there are people who truly love you aside from your accomplishments. Recognize you are not simply defined by the roles you play while you chase success, seeing that you can choose to see yourself beyond what you do and instead focus on your personal gifts, needs, and desires.

My wife is the ninth of ten kids in her family, and of those nine siblings she has, seven of them are brothers. What that means for me is, I have *a lot* of brothers-in-law. However, only one of them is an outsider like me.

Tom is the brother-in-law who is not one of my wife's brothers; instead, he is married to one of my wife's older sisters. Naturally, in the 15 years my wife and I have been married, Tom and I have always had a certain, unspoken connection: We're just there, along for the ride.

I have always appreciated the fact that Tom is a decade older than me, as it allows me to catch a glimpse of what my life might look like in ten years.

With that being said, it has been clear from the beginning that Tom's version of life will always be a bit more grandiose than mine. Because despite he and I having very similar demeanors when we are together as outsiders at family get-togethers, Tom is a solid Enneagram 3.

It is tradition that my wife's family meets up for a week in the summer at my mother-in-law's house near Sacramento. Whereas I choose to bring my work with me to help occupy my time and to ensure I am still being productive while my wife catches up with her family, Tom brings his work with him because it's such a fundamental aspect of his identity.

He's the CEO of his company. Tom is so important to so many people's livelihood that I've never once spent a week alongside him when he didn't have a constant series of meetings that he needed to be a part of for his company.

Tom is fundamentally driven by the need to be successful.

Now that I think of it, the very first time I ever heard the word "Enneagram" was from Tom years ago. He explained to me,

"When I'm hiring a new person at my company, I want to ensure I don't have two of the same Enneagram numbers on the same team. If I assess that the person I am interviewing is an 8, I know that it would not be best for the company to hire another one. *I already have an 8.* I want to curate diversity in the personalities of the people I hire, to know that I am creating the best team I can."

By now, Tom may regret ever teaching me the concept of the Enneagram because anytime he and I are together now, I always find a way to bring it into our conversation.

Last summer I asked him what he perceived his "dominant wing" to be. In case you're unfamiliar with Wings, whichever Enneagram number you are, you're also a little bit of the numbers on both sides of you. It's like an accent or a flavor to your main Enneagram number. Often, one of those "neighbors" is a bit more prominent; therefore, it is referred to as the dominant wing. (For more about Wings see pages 149-151.)

I proclaimed to Tom, "I don't see the Enneagram 4 in you, as a wing. You don't dress or act in a way that seems to stand out. Instead, you come across as very mild-mannered, conservative, and like a person who never wants to draw attention to themselves."

His response to me was enlightening: "Oh, I definitely like to stand out, but it's typically in the way I work. I always find a way to make my services and products unique in some way. I like to stand out through my successful achievements."

Spoken like a true Enneagram 3 with a dominant 4 wing.

People like Tom are in the Top 5 percentile of the ways we can arbitrarily measure success from the perspective of "The American Dream."

I am very happy for all the Enneagram 3s of the world. They work hard and earn the fruits of their accomplishments.

As for me, though, I'm completely happy being in the middle. I don't need to be one of the best; I just don't want to be one of the worst.

I can't refrain from quoting Spiderman's Uncle Ben here: "With great power comes great responsibility."

The way I see it, as someone who is not a 3, I don't desire more power or more responsibility.

Enneagram 3s thirst for success in a way that most of the rest of us cannot relate to. Every single time I've ever asked a 3 if they feel like they are competitive in everything they do, I am usually interrupted by their spouse or one of their kids:

"You don't want to play a board game or cards with him. Even if it's one that's more chance-based like *Sorry* or *Uno*, he takes it way too seriously. He always has to win. It takes the fun out of it for the rest of us!"

Does that description sound familiar? Would others say that about you? If so, you might be a 3.

Granted, a person who is constantly driving to be successful in life is naturally, by default, going to increase their overall chances of not failing; in regard to what they are setting out to accomplish.

As for me, I am happy to lose any board game or card game. I just want to be part of the group and have fun.

However, a lot of the time, I definitely look like a 3 to the outside world. Because when we 9s go into growth mode, we adopt many of the traits of an Enneagram 3.

In the chapter about Enneagram 1s, I mentioned how in my early 30s, I became very rigid, as I was in survival mode for several years; attempting to rebuild my life after my wife and I moved to

Alabama for nine months, going through all of our savings, only to have to move back to Tennessee and start over.

During those years of us having to rebuild our savings, in addition to being in tens of thousands of dollars in debt at the time, I was undeniably obsessed with work, for better and for worse.

I had a lot to prove. So much was at stake. I was forced to grow.

As an Enneagram 9, my default mode is to seek inner peace; to neither fear failure nor chase success. Safe to say, my inner peace was under attack. So, I subconsciously switched over to my growth number, which is an Enneagram 3. By doing so I was able to utilize some necessary traits that are not easily ready in my Enneagram 9 arsenal.

Sure enough, assuming the role of Enneagram 3 during that time in my life proved to be true. At least in an unspoken, subconscious sense, I did fear further failure in my life. I needed a way to make up for the lost time and the lost income that resulted from our move to Alabama.

But I found a way to dig myself out. After stumbling upon a documentary on Netflix called *Please Subscribe*, I learned that YouTubers could actually make a side income if they gained enough subscribers and views on their videos.

From there, I started watching tutorials on YouTube on how to create and edit videos, and I taught myself how to become a YouTuber. I bought some video editing software and taught myself the craft with no previous knowledge or experience.

I understood that it was not necessarily about creating content I was passionate about. Instead, the YouTube algorithm rewarded creators who consistently released material that viewers were already searching for, as YouTube is the #2 search engine in the world.

So, each day for a month, I randomly recorded three different videos about whatever random topic I could think of. By the end of those 30 days, I had created nearly a hundred videos for my library of YouTube content where I used analytic tools to determine which content was the most relevant to the free market.

One of those silly topics towered over the others when it came to the number of views: "How to Know If Your Hairline is Receding."

Believe me, I had recorded much more intelligent and thoughtful content than that in my collection. But apparently, there are enough insecure, anxious-ridden teenage boys and young men who haven't yet figured out that males are judged on their character, accomplishments, and drive more than they are on their physical appearance, beyond how they dress, and whether they have an athletic build.

Adopting an Enneagram 3 mentality, I went all in.

I began making video responses to viewers' comments. Moving forward, I recorded a minimum of 3 videos per day on the topic of "men's hair loss" for several years.

Despite having zero passion for the topic, I created a 5-step theory, and developed a quiz, to help young men predict if they would go bald. I made myself the resident expert for the topic on YouTube.

After a few years, I had set the record for having the most videos on YouTube about the subject of men's hair loss, which is well over 4,000. And actually, even now, my record still stands.

People naturally began assuming that I myself was obsessed

with the topic of men's hair loss. In reality, I was obsessed with financial security. I wanted to ensure that I was doing my part to help my family get out of debt and build our savings account.

So yes, it was ironic for a guy who still has most of his hair to be the main "hair loss guy" on YouTube. However, it is no surprise to learn that a common trait of Enneagram 3s is to create a different identity in order to make themselves seem larger than life, especially when they are put under pressure to perform.

I see a pattern in how many of the pop stars and rappers who go by a stage name, as opposed to their given name, tend to have a common theme in their lyrics: As Enneagram 3s, they remind you that they are the best: Bruno Mars, Jay-Z, and MC Hammer. And they do this through a constructed identity.

It is interesting that in our growth number, we also adopt some of the negative traits of that Enneagram number as well. In hindsight, I find the following description of the dark side of a 3 to be nothing less than prophetic, in the book, *The Enneagram Made Easy*: "They avoid feeling anxious by always being busy; may become workaholics, become reluctant to try anything new if there is any possibility of failing, take on a role or image in order to feel more secure."

That is exactly what I did for several years. A few times, I even shaved off all of my hair in an effort to be the perfect mascot for my audience.

I even openly began my videos by proclaiming myself as "The living legend of hair loss." Sure, that was a complete joke when I said that; nothing more than a tongue-in-cheek signal to the minority of my viewers who were privy enough to be in on the joke. However, it seems like the majority of my viewers took that statement as a true reflection of how I saw myself.

Ultimately, I became someone I was not. Looking back on those years, I would dub that time frame in my life as "I did what I had to do."

I'm not proud of those thousands of videos, nor am I ashamed of them. Let's be honest, I'm still sweeping in side-income from those videos I made years ago. It's gas money for my wife and me each month, even now.

These days, my videos on my YouTube channel are either about the Enneagram, or they are the songs I write. In other words, I now create content I am passionate about.

And I can afford to do that now as I am not in the financial crisis mode I was for the majority of my 30s.

Especially for men, it is specifically ingrained in us to be providers for our family, our employer, and our community.

In the book *King Warrior Magician Lover*, the Enneagram 3 male could easily be compared to the male archetype of the King.

Wrote authors Robert Moore and Douglas Gillette, "When a king became sick or weak or impotent, the kingdom languished. The rains did not come. The crops did not grow. The cattle did not reproduce. The merchants lost their trade. Drought would assault the land, and the people would perish. So, the king was the earthly conduit from The Divine World- the world of the King energy- to this world."

That's not to say women don't also carry with them a constant need to financially provide for others. But despite the concept of gender identities, I am still seeing that men specifically have this pressure on them with a greater frequency and weight.

It is typical when men meet each other for the first time, after they learn each other's names, for the next question to be, "So what do you do?" Despite it being an extremely vague question, guys know that the implied inquiry is "What do you do for a living? What's your job?"

Sure, our occupation offers insight into our natural talents, skills, and abilities, therefore showing the other person a thumbnail sketch of who we are as a man.

But there is also an unspoken "man code" in that question as well. A different way we could translate it is, "And how do you maintain a lifestyle of self-sufficiency as well as provision for those who financially depend on you?"

It is assumed that as men we are driven by this unspoken fear of losing in the game of life.

Enneagram 3s, along with their neighbors 2s and 4s, live in what's called The Shame Triad (The Heart Center); whereas 5s, 6s, and 7s occupy The Fear Triad (The Head Center), while 8s, 9s, and 1s are under The Anger Triad (The Body Center). (See Chapters 12 and 14 for more about the three Centers and the emotion Triads.)

Keep in mind that an Enneagram 3 is not only an empowering achiever, but also is undeniably influenced by his wings, Enneagram 2 (The Self-Denying Helper) and Enneagram 4 (Self-Conscious Innovator). For more on this concept check out Lauren Miltenberger's book, *Enneagram Empowerment*.

Writes Miltenberger, "Shame is a deep insecurity that who you are is not good enough. Heart-centered types address this shame in different ways: Twos, by trying to win the affection of others, Threes by trying to earn the admiration of others, and Fours by trying to embody enough individuality and uniqueness to prove their own worth to themselves."

I can imagine that to be a male Enneagram 3 is quite the paradox: You know deep down inside that people don't love you simply based on your own self-assigned measurements of success, yet others constantly remind you of your success and reinforce that image back to you.

Can you still win in the game of life while not being in first place?

Definitely. Keep in mind, there are still 8 other Enneagram types. Many of us non-3s are winning at life, but we have learned how to have more realistic expectations of what "winning" actually means.

I get it that Will Ferrell's character Ricky Bobby may have been a little too convincing in the movie *Talladega Nights*, when he said, "If you ain't first, you're last!"

But I promise you: Winning is not necessarily the opposite of losing and success is not necessarily the opposite of failure.

6

TYPE 4: THE SELF-CONSCIOUS INNOVATOR

Main Desire: To be authentic and uniquely significant

Main Fear: To be ordinary or without distinction

Go-To Hang-Up: Believing that no one understands how you feel

Path to Personal Growth: Accept that you deserve to feel joy. Acknowledge the importance of specifically naming what it is you think others have that you don't, realizing there are at least some people in your life you can trust to understand you better. Recognize that being important in others' lives does not have to be exclusive to feeling special yourself. Choose to see yourself as enough and that you might actually be fearing that others *do* understand you as opposed to not understanding you.

On September 11, 2005, I moved to Nashville, Tennessee. I was 24 years old and didn't know anyone there.

But within about a week, I managed to meet Ben, and by default, had a new best friend in the Country Music Capital of the world.

This was back in the days when you could actually drive to downtown Nashville and find a free place to park on the street. What's funny is, I don't recall one time we ever went to go see anyone perform live music in a bar.

Instead, we quickly discovered an underground ring of what I would call "professional wrestlers in humble beginnings." Every Friday night, we would gather our growing group of mutual friends to visit The Stadium Inn.

When we entered through the main door, we always tried not to laugh too hard when we saw the big white sign with large black letters that read, "NO PROSTITUTES OR DRUG DEALERS ALLOWED!".

Apparently, that was an ongoing problem for that establishment.

As for me and Ben, along with whichever friends we convinced to come and who had nothing more exciting to do on a Friday night, we were just there to see some good old fashioned American wrestling.

Despite how little money I made back then, I still always felt a little bit bad about the fact we were only charged 10 bucks for the two hours of great entertainment.

The wrestling matches were held in a banquet room. That meant when any of the wrestlers decided to jump off the ropes, they had to noticeably duck their heads in an effort to refrain from hitting the ceiling tiles.

After a few visits, we began to realize that our group of friends consisted of the only spectators who were not family members of the wrestlers. In hindsight, it did feel like we had more eyes on us than were on the wrestlers themselves.

I suppose that is part of the reason this experience became so interactive for me and Ben. Because once we realized that we were the outsiders, the only paying customers who, in the perspective of everyone else, actually believed the show was "real", we made ourselves part of the theatrics by actively trash-talking the villainous characters.

My personal favorite was a wrestler who called himself "The Polack Punisher." He always came out on stage with his slicked back long hair dripping from the bathroom sink and immediately began taunting the audience.

Ben would stand up and get his attention by yelling "yo mama" style insults, which he made up on the spot. My favorite was, "Yo mama wears combat boots... *to church!*"

I saw the look on this wrestler's face the first time he saw me holding up my sign, which presented a juvenile insult, in colorful bubble letters: "Nobody likes the Polack Punisher! He's Not Cool!"

He struggled to remain in character. He needed, in that moment, to appear to be angry. But I saw the way the corner of his mouth betrayed a smile trying not to escape.

I was right. Because a few weeks into Ben and I openly bashing The Polack Punisher, a woman approached us after the show, humbly asking, "Can I take your signs home? My husband would like to have them as souvenirs."

That's right. The Polack Punisher secretly sent his wife to us to ask for proof of our support of his craft.

Ben and I were quite the duo. Despite being in our mid 20s at the time, when we were together, it was like we were 10-year-old boys at a spend-the-night party, both of us wanting to be Michaelangelo the Ninja Turtle.

I proudly served as the buddy of an Enneagram 4. Ben was always a non-conformist. He enjoyed finding excitement out of things that most people would ignore. And he knew that I would always support him in his newest venture into absurdity.

For example, Ben found out that The Mall at Green Hills was celebrating the grand opening of a new wing. The first one hundred people who showed up that morning would receive a $50 gift card to use anywhere in the mall.

We invited our friends and we all slept in our cars. It was October, so blankets were a necessity.

Once the sun started to come up, Ben and I rushed over to be first in line. To add to the absurdity of what we were doing, he brought a TV with him and featured the movie, *Hitch*, to pass some of the wait time for everyone in line.

The Mall at Green Hills kept their word. The first hundred of us each received a $50 gift card. What I didn't realize, though, was this was Nashville's "fancy mall." There, the only thing I could afford with my $50 budget was a few Tom Petty CDs.

But I will forever treasure the memory. We were two guys who were eccentric enough to camp out for the sake of a $50 gift card. And Ben was the Enneagram 4 to initiate such a random way to spend our time.

I feel like one great big hint of an Enneagram 4 is they are often the one in your social group who always has the camera. Whether they are taking photos of nature at the nearby state park or showing up at social gatherings as if to serve as a "pop-up" photographer, 4s take time to make meaning.

What made me purchase the book, *What's Your Enneatype?* is when I saw the authors had cleverly crafted a pie chart for each Enneagram, showing which activities they specifically need the most of. For Enneagram 4, the section that took up more space than any other was labeled "Taking Time." Fortunately, there was a much-needed explanation provided:

"Non-Fours who are reading this chapter might wonder what 'taking time' means, but we bet that the FOURs reading this will completely understand. Linger, enjoy, delight in, and be present to the current moment."

I believe that in this way, Enneagram 7s are on the complete opposite end of the spectrum: Sevens want to move on to the next exciting thing, whereas 4s enjoy remaining in the moment.

One weekend, I asked Ben if he wanted to go check out my hometown of Fort Payne, Alabama. He was especially interested in learning that it is surrounded by canyons and waterfalls as the city is the gateway to the Appalachian Mountains and hosts DeSoto State Park.

For Ben, the trip to Alabama was like an amusement park. He brought his video camera and made a 6-minute "documentary" of our weekend, which he burned onto DVDs for me and our other friends that came along that weekend.

A few years later, he was the person my wife and I chose to be the videographer of our wedding.

I've never thought about it before, but I do wonder now if I would have enjoyed my move to Nashville as a 24-year-old had I not immediately befriended Ben. He undeniably brought meaning and facilitated memories being made.

I think I'm a bit partial to Enneagram 4s. I always love being around them. I am fascinated by their perspective of the world. Their presence definitely makes any experience unique.

And I feel like I'm not the only one. Consider how Bob Dylan, despite not having what most would consider a beautiful singing voice, became one of the most influential and celebrated musical performers of all time.

Enneagram 4s are definitely unique. That is not only their gift to the world but also their curse. They ultimately feel like they are not complete in some way, as if no matter what they do, they are missing something.

Another one of my favorite Enneagram 4 singer songwriters, John Mayer, has a song called "Something's Missing." He goes through a list of all the things he has which should make him feel happy, but still don't: friends, money, sleep, female companions, musical instruments, and communication with people who care about him.

Similarly, another subtle giveaway of an Enneagram 4 is that they believe they need to be rescued, and therefore, they need a rescuer.

Specifically for an Enneagram 4, they can find much growth in identifying their roles in society. As they do, 4s are able to focus less on what they don't have, which are often the things that aren't crucial to who they truly are anyway.

I always enjoy trying to identify the 4s in the crowd. Whether it's blue hair, artistic tattoo sleeves, or a snazzy pair of turquoise cowboy boots, Enneagram 4s often find a way to make their appearance stand out in the crowd, like Waldo in his signature striped red and white shirt and hat.

My 13-year-old son is an Enneagram 5 with a dominant 4 wing.

His natural choosing of "Where's Waldo?" as his Halloween costume helped me realize this. I must point out that his desire to stand out paid off; he won the overall costume contest at my wife's Halloween office party.

Enneagram 4 characters are also fun to spot in TV series and movies. I find it no coincidence that both Gene Wilder and Johnny Depp happen to be actors who played Willy Wonka, one of the most obvious displays of a male Enneagram 4, are themselves what I am calling self-conscious innovators.

If anyone could easily pass for an Enneagram 4, it would definitely be me. For most of my life, I have played guitar and written songs. I spent much of my youth acting in plays and creating my own cartoon characters. And yes, I do own a pair of turquoise cowboy boots.

Not to mention, I am the designated photographer in any social group I am part of, lugging around an actual camera and tripod!

Yet I am definitely not an Enneagram 4. I clearly remember in 5th grade, having spent my childhood during the 1980s, a time when we were constantly reminded by Saturday morning cartoon shows and by our schoolteachers that "everyone is special," that as an 11-year-old, I had the epiphany: "Wait a minute... if *everyone* is special, then *no one* can be special."

Therefore, since 1992, I have been known not to waste my time trying to feel special.

To further put this in perspective, there are currently around 8 billion people living on Earth. Sure, I've met plenty of people throughout my lifetime, but I would come nowhere close to even 1% of the world's population ever knowing who I am.

Most of the world never knew that I ever arrived on this planet. Most of them would not miss me if I was gone because they never knew I existed to begin with. And the same goes for my acknowledgement of their existence.

There is no need for me to look up at the stars to realize how small I really am. Yet still, why does it bother me that the universe without me in it wouldn't be any worse?

Am I more than just matter? Who do I matter to?

I'm invisible to billions of people, yet I don't question my existence if I know that I matter at least to some of the people who currently share this planet as their home with me.

Feeling like I matter to others helps give life meaning. It helps me feel alive and awake to our collective concept of reality.

As I mentioned, my son Jack has a dominant 4 wing, and I can easily see that in him. He cannot simply just shut off his desire to feel special and to find a rescuer.

There is a good chance he is the most intelligent person I have ever known in my entire life. But like a cat bringing the headless bodies of mice and birds they've caught and killed to the front door, my son has this habit of strategically leaving his tests on the kitchen table, always showing a 100 score, often with a note from whichever particular impressed teacher graded it.

Jack never verbally announces to my wife and I, "Hey, look at what I did. I am standing out with my perfect grades and high IQ."

Instead, he sets the stage for us to notice, and then to be the ones to verbally announce to him, which we always do: "Jack, you are so smart! That is amazing. You are definitely more intelligent than I ever was. Very impressive!"

That's his way of receiving confirmation from us that he is special.

Despite his ability to ace any test or school project, as well as his ability to effortlessly assemble the newest hopelessly impossible furniture my wife ordered, the trade-off is his needing someone to rescue him. But the identified rescuer cannot be the person who is most available to rescue him.

It's as if he seeks out people to rescue him who are more exotic and less reachable than his own completely responsible and loyal dad, who is arguably more qualified to rescue him and empathize with him than anyone else.

I regularly observe that for him, he is tuned in to his emotions way more than the rest of us in our family. I have learned to give him time and space to sort through his emotions.

This is tough for me right now, because I really don't want to use the "d-word," but it's important to embrace it, in order to understand how Enneagram 4s are wired: *Dramatic.*

It leaks out. It has been my observation that despite how well-contained and put together an Enneagram 4 can be on a regular basis, eventually they will react in a way that will make you think to yourself, *"Well, that came out of nowhere...Overreacting much?"*

Again, Enneagram 4s are some of my favorite people on the planet. Perhaps to some degree I can appreciate how they are able to be more expressive than the rest of us.

They have a way of feeling the emotions that the rest of us might turn a blind eye to, especially when it comes to those darker realities of human existence. Maybe it's not so much that they are overreacting, as it is that they are simply reacting in a way the rest of us are afraid to show.

Eventually though, when I finally realize that I have been carrying emotional burdens for so long that were never to be mine to begin with, it is often an Enneagram 4 in my life who helps me "sober up" and come to terms with what I am actually feeling.

In the same way 4s can seem to be a bit dramatic at times,

they also provide effortless therapy in any given moment, when needed.

The concept of the Enneagram teaches that, depending on which actual number we are, we typically go to another designated number for growth. While that is an important fundamental aspect of understanding how the Enneagram works, it is just as undeniable that we all experience growth in some way from each of the other numbers.

I realized just now, as I am finishing this chapter, that Enneagram 4 is my favorite aspect of my personality to explore. Seeing the world through the lens of a 4 is my version of having access to Disney World. It's my ticket to Willy Wonka's Chocolate Factory.

Sure, the original 1971 Willy Wonka movie definitely shares a lot of similarities to Netflix's series *Squid Game*, but still...

It doesn't change my fascination with the people who keep things weird and interesting and full of meaning, even when meaning is not obviously present.

7

TYPE 5: THE SELF-SUFFICIENT MINIMALIST

Main Desire: To be competent and self-sufficient

Main Fear: To be dependent or depleted

Go-To Hang-Up: Living socially detached in an effort to be self-sufficient

Path to Personal Growth: Accept that you do need other people to help you through life. Acknowledge that you do have emotions and that it is possible for you to explore them. Realize you can't do everything on your own and recognize that some people in your life are trustworthy and deserve your care. Choose to see yourself as capable.

After spending the first several years of our marriage in a

townhome on the edge of Nashville, my wife and I leveled up just in time, as we bought the last affordable new house in the "right county" due to it being rated the highest in the state for its public schools.

We were quickly introduced to a man who everyone knew as "The Mayor" of the neighborhood. After a full career of owning a variety of businesses, Ron had finally retired and decided to sell his empire in Ohio to downsize to the brand-new development where my wife and I were settling.

Despite retirement and now being in his 70s, it became immediately clear that Ron was the kind of man who can never stop working. He's the neighbor you go to when you need to borrow a ladder, or a random drill, or when you need advice on why your wife's car is making funny noises. He's also the person you call when a potentially deadly snake finds its way into your garage in the middle of July.

After I called some pest control companies and learned the exorbitant cost to remove the slithering reptile, I summoned Ron. He came over and confidently marched over to the snake (which had found shelter next to the living room entry in the garage) and promptly declared, "Ehh, that's just an ole corn snake. Hand me a rake."

Without saying another word, he effortlessly captured the snake, then asked me, "Where do you want me to put it?"

I wasn't sure if that was a trick question. What were my options? How far was he willing to carry it away?

Whatever mumbled response I gave him, he headed into the wooded area beyond our neighborhood to release the non-poisonous snake.

That's the relationship I've had with Ron in the near decade he and I have been neighbors–I seek the help of the self-sufficient minimalist. He immediately helps me, which solves my problem, while undeniably proving how self-sufficient he is.

More recently, Ron was walking his dog one morning as I was out waiting with my daughter for her bus. As is his tradition, he asked me, "So what trouble have you got yourself into this time?"

I mentioned to him how my dad had just helped me replace the shower head and light fixture in our master bathroom.

Ron responded with a bit of a chuckle: "Well, let me ask you something. When are you going to start figuring out how to do some of this stuff yourself?"

As if attempting to gain the approval of a strict schoolteacher, I explained, "Actually, not too long ago, I was able to replace a part of our clothes dryer after watching a few videos on YouTube."

The look he gave me seemed to say, "I'm not impressed. You've got a long way to go." But instead of actually speaking those words out loud, he chose not to waste his energy.

In typical Ron tradition, he simply walked away while shaking his head.

Right now, in your mind, I want you to picture a person who always seems to be slightly grumpy, never seems to need anyone else's help, *and* is clearly the smartest person in the room. There's a good chance you've just identified an Enneagram 5 in your life.

My official title for the Enneagram 5 is "Self-Sufficient Minimalist." By default, people with this personality type are out to prove to the world and to themselves that they don't really need others. They have themselves, and that's all they need in order to make it through life.

(And now the Hank Williams Jr. song, "A Country Boy Can Survive," is playing in my head.)

I like to joke that all 5s are somewhere on the "hoarder spectrum." My 13-year-old son who is a true 5 is currently hoarding Nike tennis shoes, empty bottles of Prime energy drinks, and unopened packages of Hot Wheels that he believes will one day be worth a lot of money.

He also hoards knowledge of sport cars. We can't drive anywhere as a family without randomly hearing a shout from the back seat: "Oh! Look! It's a brand-new Porsche 911 with..." The details he rattles out beyond that always remind me of how in the classic 1983 movie, *A Christmas Story*, Ralphie makes everyone aware of the one thing on his wish list:

"An official Red Ryder, carbine action, 200-shot, range model air rifle, with a compass in the stock and this thing that tells time..."

Mainly, Enneagram 5s are naturally drawn to hoarding knowledge on particular subjects. Second, they are naturally drawn to proactively overstocking supplies. If you plan on surviving the zombie apocalypse, you'll definitely want to buddy up with a 5.

Enneagram 5s are known for seeing their home as their private fortress, to which they like to retreat from the world and work on their craft.

They have a natural instinct to preserve their resources—whether it's their physical energy, their social capacity, or their material possessions. Their main fear is to be dependent or depleted.

A 5 is more inclined to live with a scarcity mindset, causing them to constantly fear that there will never be enough, and they must therefore conserve their resources; as opposed to an abundance mindset, which teaches there is always enough.

Right now, I can't stop thinking about Batman as a prime

example of a 5, even down to all 3 instincts, which every Enneagram represents to some degree: the self-preservation, the social, and the sexual. (See pages 154–160 about the 3 Instincts.)

Batman's Self-Preservation instinct of an Enneagram 5 is apparent, as he focuses on minimizing his needs and limits their access to others by building boundaries: Batman has his secret Bat Cave where he creates and stores all his self-sufficient gadgets.

Since the Social instinct focuses on a particular moral code, Batman can understandably be confused with an Enneagram 1.

Even the Sexual instinct presents itself in Batman, as most superheroes (or vigilantes, in this case) are not known for having a designated sidekick. This instinct focuses on working with a partner, which he finds in Robin.

Batman is an investigator. He's basically a freelance detective. Not only does he figure out on his own who the current villain is and their particular plot device, but he brings his own hand-crafted weapons to the fight! (Cue Jack Nicholson's Joker saying, "Where does he get those wonderful toys?")

Seriously, how is Batman not the epitome of what it means to be a Self-Sufficient Minimalist?

Well, Indiana Jones comes to mind, too. Often mistaken for an action hero, in the same way Batman is mistaken for a superhero (he has no superpowers), Indiana Jones is more of a clever detective, yet a bumbling fighter. He just happens to look really cool when he snaps his whip!

Indiana Jones is simply an archeology professor who enjoys treasure hunting, with the goal of adding relics to his collection in a museum. He is not a hero. The only people he "saves" are his token partners in each of the movies who he ultimately puts in danger through his own personal quests for ancient trophies.

Also allow me to point out the fact that Indiana Jones himself never actually seems to defeat the villain. Instead, he typically leads them to every treasure he is hunting, then allows them to be destroyed by its power, because conveniently, the villain always wants the treasure for more selfish reasons than Indiana Jones.

And I can't talk about fictional famous 5s without mentioning one of the most beloved sitcom characters in the past few decades who just happens to share the same first name as my previously mentioned neighbor: Ron Swanson from *Parks and Rec.*

Most of Ron's dialogue revolves around him openly declaring he doesn't need people and that he can take care of himself, like when he goes to the building supply store and immediately rejects the help of a worker by replying, "I know more than you."

One of the ways I can look like a Five is the fact I do not like people beyond my immediate family to be inside my home. I am very private when it comes to my personal space. I always laugh every time my wife buys some new flag or sign for our front porch with the word "Welcome."

I always ask her, "Who's that for?" Anyone who would have to walk up to our front door and read that sign is immediately someone who is specifically not welcome in my house. The only people who are welcome are the ones who would come through the garage door instead, meaning me, her, and our kids.

But if you were somehow an exception to the rule and found a golden ticket to visit my house through the private garage door entrance (the way the non-poisonous corn snake tried to enter), you would notice the wall next to my Jeep.

That is my "bunker wall," where I overstock my groceries that won't fit inside the kitchen. Typically, you would randomly find a few boxes of seltzer water, containers of protein powder, and jars of sauerkraut.

Whenever there is a 2-for-1 special at the grocery store, I am known for buying all of the remaining inventory, whether it's cottage cheese, yogurt, or bacon. I will find a way to make space for it in one of the drawers in our fridge.

One of the proposed spirit animals of Enneagram 5 is a hamster. Our family has kept Syrian hamsters as pets, so I can confirm that a hamster embodies an Enneagram 5.

They are solitary creatures: You cannot keep more than one in the same cage, as they need their own space to burrow into wood shavings to build tunnels to hoard their food.

Unlike dogs, hamsters do not demand attention or seek companionship. Instead, they are self-sufficient, beyond you giving them food and water, and occasionally letting them out of their home to run around for a few minutes and explore a different environment. Anything beyond that and they become depleted of physical energy and are ready to return to their home of solitude and supplies.

Yes, I am aware of the perceived paradox in which a minimalist may have an instinct for hoarding. Now that I think of it, I'm sure each of the nine types presents its own contradictory concept:

Enneagram Ones often live by such strict standards in the pursuit of achieving perfection that they eventually begin to break their own rules.

Twos are known for helping others, but not for helping themselves.

Threes can fear failure to the point where they avoid risks that would lead them to success.

Fours place themselves in a contest to prove they are unique, in a world full of 8 billion people who are already special in their own ways.

Sixes are the loyal skeptics, having more doubt *and* more faith than the other Enneagram types.

Sevens have a habit of not finishing the many projects they start, though completing those tasks could actually be what helps actually quench their FOMO.

Eights want to remain in control, despite the reality that most things in life are actually out of our control.

Nines are often the best negotiators, despite their driving desire to avoid conflict or confrontation whenever they can.

We are layered and complex people. We should give ourselves the grace to recognize that all of us have our own peculiar messes to sort through.

In the post-Covid shutdown world, I am one who prefers life as it is now. I love not having to drive into an office and work next to people.

For over three years now, my office has been my kitchen table, which is only a few feet away from the refrigerator and the bathroom and has an impeccable view out the window into my backyard (which is currently a corn field). It is everything I need, and I am so much happier there than I ever was driving an hour in traffic to work alongside people who, as much as I loved being around them, ultimately distracted me from doing my job.

When I do leave my house, the few places I visit are all within a three-mile radius of my house: my gym, my grocery store, and my church. This concept is comforting to me.

What is not comforting to me is being at a place like Disney World, which instantly transforms me into a bitter old man:

"I hate crowds. I hate lines. I hate paying too much for everything. I hate the Most Magical Place on Earth."

I'll get into this more later, but I was a very shy little boy. I was the ultimate introvert. Overcoming my fear of social interaction would ultimately lead me to becoming the most outgoing extrovert most people *think* they know.

Fives are by default, the official introverts of the Enneagram spectrum wheel. If you see yourself as a private person who feels drained by social interaction, you may have a 5 as one of your wings, or you may actually be an Enneagram 5.

A quick word from Ramon: The research confirms it as does my experience as a couple's therapist: A Type 5 is much more likely to be a male. By nature, regardless of where she is on the introversion/extroversion spectrum, a core relational value and need for a woman is connection—connection with her family, with her partner, with her children, with her friends. This certainly doesn't mean that men don't desire and need connection; it simply means that the need and value of connection tends to be higher for women. I've written an entire chapter about the contrasting needs and the corresponding fears that men and women have in my upcoming book *Spooning with a Fork: How to Be a Couple.*

I'm pointing this out here in the chapter on Type 5 because if you're a Type 5 guy, you likely face a dilemma in your close relationship with a woman and it is this: How do you help your wife feel close and connected to you (through conversation, shared activities, and touch) when you tend to have less of a need for all three points of connection than she does? By the way, the same dilemma exists for you if you're the father of a daughter.

Space in this chapter doesn't permit a detailed solution to your dilemma, but I'll remind you of one of the guiding principles about the Enneagram in close relationships that I mentioned in Chapter 2, specifically the balance of Acceptance and Adjustment and the exchange of Meaningful and Manageable. As a Five you are naturally independent and self-sufficient, possessing a need for solitude to complete tasks, process your world, and to recharge your battery. You will just have to be careful and not allow a healthy measure of solitude to become something your spouse and children experience as withdrawal or isolation.

And now, back to Nick: One final fundamental trait of 5s is the need to secretly have the answers but not necessary to "be right." Whereas Enneagram 1s typically claim to know they have the truth, and the correct answers that everyone else needs to live by, a 5 doesn't necessarily have a desire to reform others to their perception of reality.

Instead, a typical Enneagram 5 will spend as much time and energy as it takes to research the most logical solution and then live by it without needing anyone else's approval or confirmation.

I can easily imagine a 5 being the person who knew the answer all along and when someone else in the group finally discovers this, they ask the 5 why they didn't tell everyone sooner. The 5 would calmly reply, "Well, nobody asked me."

Since Enneagram 5s are driven by a desire to be perceived as competent, it implies that an easy way to trigger a 5 is to imply they are incompetent. Though 5s may not be seen as emotional as the rest of the group, to attack their competence is a way to trigger them into stress mode.

Fives make such an effort to not look foolish, which is why

they are so diligent in their research–to become the most knowledgeable in the areas they do speak about.

I would theorize this is a reason a majority of male comedians are 6s, as opposed to 5s, as 5s would naturally avoid even the appearance of self-deprecation, even for a laugh.

Meanwhile, 6s find comfort in being able to publicly excuse themselves from the pressure of having to seem like they have all the answers.

Similarly, I have noticed it is also much less common for a 5 to be a singer-songwriter or a frontman in a band, as opposed to a 6. Although Ramon has noted that in his counseling work here in Nashville, he has met a number of touring musicians and singers who are quite expressive and demonstrative on stage but who are introverts off-stage. A lead singer of a well-known band told Ramon, "That guy on stage is a persona. I get to be an actor playing a character. It's fun. But frankly, I hate those Meet & Greet things before or after a show. Before a concert, I'm focused on the show about to start. After a concert, I'm physically and emotionally exhausted, and I wish everyone would leave me alone, including my bandmates. I bet a lot of fans are disappointed after meeting me, probably saying to a friend, "I thought he would be friendlier."

You don't have to be a Type 5 concert artist to dread a Meet & Greet. If you're a Type 5 entrepreneur or if you work in a corporate environment, then few things strike fear and dread into you like a networking event. Your idea of eternal torment is a never-ending networking event in a hotel ballroom prior to the conference. Stand, mingle and chat; stand, mingle and chat, with no end ever in sight and nothing to eat but cheap hors d'oeuvres. A Type 7's heaven is a Type 5's hell.

Do you personally relate to what makes up a Self-Sufficient Minimalist? If Batman, Indiana Jones, and Ron Swanson are much more relatable to you than Spiderman, Han Solo, and Ron Burgandy, then you might be the self-sufficient investigator.

And if you are, I'm confident you won't be announcing your Enneagram number the next time you're at a social gathering. No, that's the Enneagram 6's job, as he is always looking for confirmation of his identity and his role in society.

You'll see what I mean in the next chapter...

8

TYPE 6: THE SELF-DOUBTING TROUBLESHOOTER

Main Desire: To feel safe, secure, and supported

Main Fear: To be unprepared, unstable, and to not have reassurance

Go-To Hang-Up: Living in anxiety, seeing life as one big collective existential crisis

Path to Personal Growth: Accept that you can trust yourself and acknowledge that your sharp instinct will guide you even when your well-crafted plans don't always work out. Realize you can address your fear in a healthy way by choosing to see it as a challenge to overcome. Recognize that your trust in yourself, in your community, and in your systems have taught you it's going to be okay. Choose to see yourself as not only belonging but as a backbone to your social groups.

One sloppy Saturday morning, I happened to randomly take my 7-year-old daughter to Kohl's to help me shop for some cool new t-shirts. I chose one with Bob Dylan, to which she commented, "He looks a little bit bumpy." I didn't even bother with a follow-up question as somehow I think I knew what she meant.

She then saw one featuring The Mystery Machine, along with that famous group of crime-solving teens and their mostly English-speaking Great Dane.

Later that day, due to my 13-year-old son wanting to binge-watch *Young Sheldon*, our household ended up getting HBO Max. As I apathetically scrolled through the offerings of yet another streaming channel, I noticed *Scooby-Doo, Where Are You!* was included in our subscription.

As you can imagine, it didn't take long before my daughter and I started watching back-to-back episodes of the TV show, based on the t-shirt she chose for me at Kohl's.

Her immediate observation after the first episode was this: "Daddy, Shaggy is the most scared out of everyone, but he still tries to have fun."

Yes, my 7-year-old daughter actually described what it means to be an Enneagram 6 with a dominant 7 wing.

Enneagram 6s can be very difficult to identify. I would know, because I spent over a year believing I was a *Counterphobic* Enneagram 6.

I finally discovered my true identity when my anxiety got so intense that I decided to Google "ways to cure anxiety". That led me to a self-assigned experiment where I cut my daily caffeine intake in half. Within a week, all of my anxiety magically cleared up, and it hasn't returned since.

So, if you think you might be an Enneagram 6, try life without caffeine for a while. You might find that you are actually an Enneagram 9 like me, who is constantly living in their stress Enneagram number of 6, due to the stress hormone, cortisol, which can be heightened due to caffeine consumption.

If you still think you might be a 6, then it's important to differentiate the three instincts (see pages 154-160), since they are the most diverse of all nine Enneagram numbers. To further illustrate this, it is mandatory I talk about *Star Wars.*

Imagine the anxiety-riddled C3PO, who is constantly verbalizing what might go wrong, modeling the Self-Preservation instinct that can resemble a 2.

Now consider the loyal and adventurous Chewbacca, or the confident yet code-abiding Obi-Wan Kenobi; they are both the Social instinct that can resemble a 1 or 3.

And lastly, consider the terror-inducing Darth Vader, who faced his fears by turning to The Dark Side, after his dedication to The Force failed to save his wife's life while she was giving birth to his twins. Darth Vader is one of the most legendary examples of the Sexual instinct, or Counterphobic 6, that can resemble an 8.

Let's take a glimpse at three different guys I know who are 6s, each of whom have a different instinct.

Josh always initiates the conversation with his ongoing concerns with the *perpetually doomed* weather, the *perpetually doomed* economy, and the *perpetually doomed* political situation of our nation. It's as if he's trying to recruit me to agree with him about his worries, to give him assurance that I am truly part of his tribe and support system. He is a phobic self-preservation 6, who most resembles C3Po.

Aaron is known as the funny guy. He's a self-proclaimed dork who loves to joke about his favorite drink of choice being White Claw, which is comically ironic for a man who is 6' 8". While he definitely appears carefree and jolly on the outside, he has revealed to me that he is constantly dealing with anxiety on the inside, so he focuses on serving the group's needs–in his case, as the court jester. He is a social 6, who most resembles Chewbacca or Obi-Wan Kenobi.

Bryan has a slight obsession with guns and self-defense. He has a concealed weapon permit and even practices martial arts. He drives a big black Jeep Wrangler with off-roading tires. Like my friend Josh, he also finds a way to drive the conversation back to things that are largely out of his control, like the weather, economy, and politics. However, Bryan addresses his anxiety about these topics in a way that conveys that he somehow has control, as opposed to being controlled. He is a counterphobic sexual 6 who most resembles Darth Vader.

If 6s are largely identified by their anxiety, I want to point out that it does have a plus side wherein anxiety may serve as "problem-solving fuel."

The possible negative outcomes in the room are constantly presenting themselves. The social tension between the people around you is overwhelming.

You are living in the past, as you keep in mind what life has taught you through a countless number of experiences, as well as the future, as you are forecasting the outcome with decent accuracy, and as you are simultaneously living in the present, trying to get by.

Your brain is constantly trying to put together puzzle pieces to "solve all the problems" at the same time.

This concept is further complicated by the concept that Enneagram 6s are caught between their two very opposing wings: a more pessimistic, introverted 5; and a more optimistic, extroverted 7.

Are 6s pessimistic introverts or optimistic extroverts?

The answer: Yes! *All the time.*

Sixes have to be, in order to try to fulfill their main desire of belonging and being supported, and in order to face their main fear of being unprepared, unstable, and not having reassurance.

You recognize Gandhi's famous quote: "Be the change you wish to see in the world."

For Enneagram 6s, instead it's, "Be the *stability* you wish to see in the world."

In the same way that Enneagram 3s typically fear failure, and as a result, tend not to fail as often as the rest of us, Enneagram 6s typically fear lack of stability, and therefore, become the backbone of their social environment.

Despite their never-ending struggle with uncertainty, as well as maybe even secretly taking a hit on their self-confidence because of it, Enneagram 6s suddenly become very certain and self-confident when an actual threat presents itself.

Strangely enough, it's as if 6s experience a sense of relief and even comfort in the chaos, since that is what they are constantly designed to handle!

Sometimes they will instinctively prove how *not afraid* they are, which reveals that fundamentally, they are motivated by the fear of instability.

I often find this trait in Enneagram 6 actors who tend to play the

NICK SHELL & RAMON PRESSON

"unassuming leader/accidental hero" in a majority of their movie roles: Chuck Norris, Steven Seagal, Ben Affleck, Robert De Niro, Mark Wahlberg, and Tommy Lee Jones.

The characters they play tend to live by a sure-fire 3-step strategy: warn everyone of the threat of pending doom, recruit a network of competent helpers, and then initiate the rescue of the people who were unable to escape in time.

We don't tend to think of Tom Hanks as an "action star," but even when voicing the character of Woody in the *Toy Story* series, his Enneagram 6 vibes are undeniable.

But just as a word of caution: you might want to avoid traveling with Tom Hanks, because things are probably going to get a lot worse before he can make them better. See *Cast Away*, *Apollo 13*, *Captain Phillips*, *Sully*, and *Greyhound* as evidence.

Sixes are loyal to their people. They are responsible and hard-working. If the ship they are on is sinking, they are going to use their problem-solving skills to keep everyone alive and find a way to be rescued. And if there is no way out, they accept their fate of going down with the ship, and warmly help others around them cope with their shared fate.

Enneagram 6s are often calm in a crisis. It's just the rest of their lives when there is no chaos to control, that they feel like everything is falling apart, at least on the inside.

It is often 6s who fill in those awkward pauses the moment they present themselves in a group conversation.

It is often 6s who remind everyone of that very important detail for the project that slipped everyone else's mind.

It is often 6s who are the first to notice a pattern, then craft a five-step plan that they then share with the others on how to not only fix the problem, but to prevent it from happening again.

Keep in mind that whichever Enneagram type you are, you rotate between the three Instincts as needed. (See pages 154-160 for detailed explanation about Instincts.) So for a 6, you may start your day by leaning on Self-Preservation which focuses on making social connections to be protected. By the afternoon, your Social instinct might take the wheel and focuses on the rules and guidelines to follow, for fear of doing wrong in the eyes of authorities. And by evening, you may tap into your Sexual instinct and focus on facing your fear directly by assuming a strong alter-ego, in an attempt to deny your fears.

Those easily sound like three different people, which redirects us back to the fact that each Enneagram Type has three instincts. Most of us also have a most dominant instinct, followed by our back-up instinct, and then what I call our "blind spot" instinct.

A 6 with the Sexual instinct has an agenda to build one-on-one relationships with people. They are that guy who constantly talks to strangers wherever they go. It's their subconscious attempt to further build their social network, therefore giving them a greater sense of stability and security.

A 6 with the Social instinct has an agenda to cater to the needs of the group they are a part of at that moment. This is where their people-pleasing nature is perhaps most evident as both a strength and a weakness.

In both of these instincts, if a 6 has a counterphobic tendency, they seem to take pride in establishing themselves as the outsider, making that the reason people should trust them. The concept being, "I do things differently. I found a better way. I'll take you under my wing and talk you through it."

The psychology behind this is that they are facing their fears of not belonging to society by openly identifying as someone who doesn't want to "fit in."

It is no surprise that the Social instinct of an Enneagram 4 focuses on how much they are suffering and is often mistaken as a 6.

And that brings me to another nuance about 6s– they make great songwriters!

I have been writing songs for over 30 years. For me, I suppose it's always been a form of therapy for me, to put down in words what is actually going on inside my head. It's a way of materializing the subconscious and the unknown in a way I can address it.

Looking back on the dozens of songs I've written, most of which were written years before I knew anything about the Enneagram, the fact I go to a 6 in stress was always present in my lyrics, particularly in the themes of self-discovery and ultimately in the pursuit of finding belonging and security.

I was both surprised and relieved to learn that so many popular musicians were an Enneagram 6 all along.

Bruce Springsteen's catalogue is largely composed of songs identifying himself as an outsider who just wants someone to join him in an "us against the world" mentality, in classics like "Born to Run", "Thunder Road," and "Dancing in the Dark".

Tom Petty continually established himself as a Counterphobic 6 who struggles to belong, while openly facing his fears in songs like, "Even the Losers," "Learning to Fly," and "Runnin' Down a Dream."

James Hetfield has basically written the soundtrack for what Counterphobic 6 means while Metallica's 1991 untitled "Black Album" consists of dark anthems including "Enter Sandman," "Sad but True," and "Through the Never."

A few years later in 1994, Billie Joe Armstrong made it cool to struggle with anxiety while desperately seeking a sense of security, with Green Day's legendary album, *Dookie*, containing "Basket Case," "Welcome to Paradise," and "She."

Bono, of U2, is constantly focused on working towards reconciliation through compromise in an effort to gain a feeling of security, in songs like "With or Without You," "One," and "Sweetest Thing."

Jon Bon Jovi repeatedly penned hit singles based on his desire to feel connection with another person, while facing the odds with them and/or against them in "Livin' on a Prayer," "It's My Life," and "Always."

Dan Reynolds of Imagine Dragons seems obsessed with self-improvement as he explores and unpacks the guilt and shame he represses found in his self-preservation instinct, while at the same time looking to overcome his anxiety and fears as revealed in songs like "Believer," "Thunder," and "Whatever It Takes,"

Eminem was the best-selling artist of the 2000s and the best-selling male artist of the 2010's. He is perhaps one of the most famous (and infamous) Counterphobic 6s in entertainment history, as he constantly reminds us with purposely shocking lyrics in #1 hits like "My Name Is," "The Real Slim Shady," and "Without Me."

In my chapter about Enneagram 3s, I alluded to my steady workout routine. I'm typically at the gym three to six days per week, where I do an hour of compound exercises. For my lunch hour, instead of eating food like a normal person, I go on a one-hour walk, no matter the weather, sometimes while carrying a backpack filled with the weights (also known as rucking).

Yes, I'm convinced everyone in my surrounding neighborhood thinks I'm crazy. I don't blame them.

But this is something I do to quiet any potential anxiety as the day begins, by having a time and space to think through the constant stream of problems I am trying to solve in my head while becoming stronger, and feeling stronger, as a means to both symbolically and literally overcome my fears.

After a friend recently asked me about my current weight training routine, he immediately followed up with, "Who are you working out with? I noticed you kept saying *we* instead of I."

His question surprised and confused me. I had no idea I was using plural pronouns exclusively when referencing what I do at the gym.

Two weeks later, I saw him again and proudly shared the much-anticipated answer to his question: "Okay, I figured it out. Using the term "we" was my subconscious's way of acknowledging that my daily workouts are the specific time each day when my mind and body truly feel connected. It's the perfect aid to mental health and physical health. It makes me feel alive, in control, and calm."

Think back to a Top 10 favorite guys' movie of all time: *Fight Club.*

The main character, who technically goes unnamed, is an openly Phobic 6, who creates a tougher version of himself, known as Tyler Durden, a clear Counterphobic 6.

Even as a young boy, I always identified with He-Man and Battle Cat, as both of them were openly phobic until granted the mysterious Power of Grayskull to which they magically become confident, powerful beasts!

However, as I grew into my teenage years, life itself seemed to confirm a theory—that perhaps I didn't need the Power of

Grayskull in order to transform. I eventually developed a secret motto to live by, which has served as a major life hack for me, and it is this: "No one else can tell the difference between me pretending to be sure of myself and actually being sure of myself." If any Enneagram could adopt "Fake it 'til you make it!" as their motto, I would say it would be 6s.

I'm imagining the Enneagram 6 of the show *Friends* right now, Chandler Bing: "Could I *be* any more sure of myself?"

It turns out that Enneagram 6 happens to be the most common type among comedians, especially talk show hosts: Johnny Carson, Jay Leno, Jon Stewart, Jimmy Kimmel, Seth Meyers, Ben Stiller, Larry David, Sebastian Maniscalco, Louis C.K., Neil Brennan, Chris Farley, and Chris Rock, to name more than a few.

Take note of the underlying awkwardness in the way that David Letterman always delivers his jokes and conducts his interviews. There is an unashamed dorkiness about him, which happens to make the male Enneagram 6s particularly funny.

So, despite all the struggles with anxiety and belonging, there's definitely a plus side. In addition to being very consistent and dependable people, 6s can be funny.

I find it fascinating that overcoming the uncertainties in life means that a person develops a sense of humor, which therefore helps them relate and connect to society, therefore increasing their sense of security in the world.

Typically, 6s are traditionally known as the Loyal Skeptics, but I believe they are so much more than that. They are even more than my title for 6s– the Self-Doubting Troubleshooter.

They are the backbones of society. They figure out how to stabilize the situation. They are the ones who stick around and will go down with the ship if they have to. Along the way, they will make you sing and make you laugh...even if on the inside, they are caught up in a thunderstorm of uncertainty and chaos.

Some of the features of an Enneagram 6 are simply an undeniable aspect of the human experience, no matter which Enneagram type you actually are. Can you see aspects of the 6 in yourself?

None of us really know what we are doing here. It's something we have to figure out.

None of us really know what's ahead. We are all looking for a sense of security in the unknown, forming an alliance of people we trust and depend on as we continually form and maintain a network of social security.

It reminds me of my first day of kindergarten. My mom told me, "Nick, just look for anyone you already know, maybe from preschool. You're not the only one feeling this way. I'm sure there are other kids looking to you in the same way you need them."

Those are legendary words of wisdom from my mom in 1986. They were true then and they are true now, for us all.

We're all faking it until we make it.

But for 6s specifically, they question whether they've actually made it... and then they are skeptical for how long it will even last.

9

TYPE 7: THE SELF-DRIVEN VARIETY SEEKER

Main Desire: To be happy by exploring new opportunities and a variety of adventures

Main Fear: To feel trapped or stuck

Go-To Hang-Up: Living in fear of missing out and in fear of experiencing pain and/or boredom

Path to Personal Growth: Accept that what you may actually be in fear of missing out on is stability and contentment. Acknowledge that it is not fair to you for others to always rely on you for their entertainment. Realize it is important for you to experience negative emotions and the darker themes of life. Recognize that it's not the events themselves you fear missing out on; rather it's the people who show up to your life. Choose to see yourself as complete instead of empty.

While perfectly healthy in the prime of his life, a man decides to plan his own funeral. He prefers to get it all out of the way now, so he won't have to think about death while he is still alive.

So, the man books a U-Haul to pull all his belongings behind the hearse. He goes all out on purchasing his casket, making sure it will be the latest model, with all the bells and whistles, including Wi-Fi, of course. It goes without saying, he will be burying all of his money with him, six feet deep.

As for his memorial service, he ensures that all of his guests will be well taken care of and entertained. After all, it's important to him that his funeral gets 5-star reviews. There will be a salad bar, a variety of food trucks, and a giant chocolate fondue fountain.

Between the waterslide and the bounce house and the pony rides, who could possibly be sad at his funeral?!

Never does it occur to this man that he will not actually be there to see anyone enjoy his amazing send-off. That's because this fictional man I created to open this chapter is none other than a cartoonish version of an Enneagram 7.

Of all the Enneagram books I have read over the years, I have yet to find one that quotes Chris Traeger from *Parks and Rec*, from the episode, "Bus Tour", as he makes a sobering confession to the camera crew: "If I keep my body moving and my mind occupied at all times, I will avoid falling into a bottomless pit of despair."

I'm no Enneagram 7, but man, can I adopt that as my life verse?

Whereas one of my grandfathers was the stereotypical Enneagram 1, my other grandfather was the complete opposite.

With the Self-preservation instinct of an Enneagram 7, Papaw Shell was the textbook definition of a "rolling stone".

I am completely convinced that so much of what inspired my dad to become such a loyal and hardworking man was due to him needing to step in and be a father to his younger sisters during the months-at-a-time his own father was out of the picture. It reminds me a lot of the concept behind the Johnny Cash song, "Boy Named Sue". (*More on my dad in the next chapter about Type 8s.*)

Though he lived less than an hour away from me, I have no memories of Papaw Shell ever coming to visit me for Thanksgiving, Christmas, my birthdays, or even my wedding. However, he did make some notably generous contributions to me personally throughout my life:

For my 8th birthday, I happened to be in Chattanooga where he lived. Out of nowhere, he presented me with a Honda Spree moped. And I have to say that special gift had a fundamental effect on my childhood development. Being able to drive around on that motor scooter and explore surrounding neighborhoods was one of the highlights of my boyhood.

Papaw Shell's gift of freedom and adventure undeniably further unlocked so much of the Enneagram 7 in me. Many years later at age 15, I was at his house for Christmas and casually mentioned to him how for my first car I really wanted a car that was a 1983 model. He opened up the newspaper and turned to the classifieds. By that afternoon, he had bought me a 1983 BMW 320i.

There was no question about it. That was one cool car to drive to school when I turned 16, with its burgundy leather seats, fancy sunroof, and actual wood panel interior.

When I graduated college, becoming the first person in my

entire family tree to do so, Papaw Shell presented me with a most appropriate gift as I made my move to Nashville, Tennessee: a Martin DM Mahogany Dreadnought guitar.

Not only is it the nicest guitar I have ever owned, but I still continue to write all my songs on it, which are featured on my YouTube channel.

I fully recognize my dad's relationship with Papaw was completely different. But for me, I only knew Papaw Shell as a kind, friendly, laid-back man who loved to tell jokes. He owned a baseball cap that read, "When in doubt... *mumble.*" Seriously, that is hilarious.

When a person entered the room, he immediately acknowledged them as if they were a celebrity. It was hard to hide in a corner when Papaw Shell was there.

Never did I have any negative feelings toward him, despite him not showing up in my life in the more traditional ways a grandfather would be there for his grandson. When he passed away several years ago, I immediately began crying at his funeral, along with the rest of his grandsons. (And I don't cry at funerals!)

Papaw Shell had definitely reached me. He made me feel special. And he undeniably brought out a side of me that wasn't there before.

Also during my childhood, another Enneagram 7 served as a heavy influence on me "coming out of my shell." *(Pun intended: My last name is Shell.)*

It's extremely difficult for anyone to imagine now, but as a young boy, I was constantly harassed by the general public with questions like, "What's the matter, cat got your tongue?" and "You're too shy! Why don't you ever talk?" After years of that narrative being presented to me, it made me feel like I didn't matter in life unless I had something to say.

Fortunately, an unknown playwright named Eddie McPherson showed up in my preteen years and personally asked me to take on a small, non-speaking role in the newest play he had just written. Sure, I was terrified, but he was able to convince me: "All I need you to do is to pretend like you're collecting seashells at the front of the stage, to make it seem like everyone is at a beach..."

The next year, Eddie had written a new play, and recruited me again: "All I need you to do is to say a few lines and let people chase you around on stage for an action scene..."

And the year after that: "All I need you to do is be one of the main characters and sing one of the songs..."

Eventually, I was in every play I could audition for, whether it was at church, at school, or as part of my town's drama program while school was out.

Gaining so much experience acting had subconsciously taught me what Steve Martin explained to Jerry Seinfeld in Season 7, Episode 2 of *Comedians in Cars Getting Coffee*:

"When I first started, I decided it was important to fake confidence. Because I thought it was important that [the audience] sensed I believed. If I was the slightest bit nervous about something, they could smell it, and then they would become judges. But if I was confident, it's like 'I don't care what you think.' That worked."

By the time I was in 7th grade, drawing from the new confidence I gained through acting in all those plays, I learned to play the guitar and write songs.

One specific memory I have of Eddie undeniably proving he was an Enneagram 7 was when our church youth group travelled to Panama City Beach for a Spring Break Retreat. By that point, Eddie had become the youth minister.

On the way there, we stopped at McDonald's for lunch. After they finished eating, several of the kids in the youth group made their way out to the indoor playground. The manager began to take notice of all the kids who were too old to be playing on the equipment. Suddenly, he burst through the door to the indoor playground and demanded, "Who is in charge here?!"

On cue, 33-year-old Eddie McPherson slid out the bottom of the tube slide to reluctantly declare: *"I am?"*

If it weren't for Papaw Shell and my playwright mentor Eddie McPherson, both of whom happened to be Enneagram 7s, it's hard to imagine that I, as a shy little boy, would have ended up down the variety-seeking and adventurous path of acting, and by my teen years and beyond, traveling the world.

By the time I was 17, I had started an impressive stamp collection...on my passport, that is. I spent time performing drama, singing, playing guitar, teaching, and exploring Ecuador, Trinidad and Tobago, Thailand, Korea, and New Zealand.

That's quite a character arc, if you ask me! So much for being shy.

If I were given a Native American name now, it would surely be "Must Talk to Strangers". I have no fear of public speaking. Instead, I have a fear of *not* public speaking!

As a young boy, I was made to feel like I didn't matter in life unless I had something to say. Problem solved: I now *always* have something to say.

I am fortunate that the Enneagram 7 men who inspired me were adventurous, whether or not they realized how forever impactful they would be to my life.

In some alternative timeline where I never discovered those character-building interests, would I still be that quiet, reserved person I was back in the 1980s? Would I even be writing this book that you are reading now? I honestly believe I would be a much different person.

By the time I got to college, I could have easily passed as an Enneagram 7. So much so, that I was halfway through my college career before I even knew what I should major in, *or in theory, what I wanted to be when I grew up.*

What was that one thing I was passionate enough to commit to for the rest of my life as a career?

As I was effortlessly cranking out a 10-page term paper one night, I overheard some of my dormmates make a comment: "Oh... that reminds me. I need to start on my stupid essay for English. I hate writing those. They are the hardest part about college!"

That's when it hit me: Writing long papers was the *easiest* part about college for me. I had a talent for getting perfect scores on papers I wrote, even if I never actually read the book I was writing about!

Meanwhile, math and science were a constant struggle for me. But by my senior year of college, by the time I got all those silly math and science classes out of the way, I graduated on the Dean's List with a 4.3 GPO... *as an English major.*

A couple of decades later, I still use that example as what inspired one of my many life mottos, which happens to rhyme: "The things that you're bad at? *Avoid 'em.* The things that you're good at? *Exploit 'em."*

Life is hard, and therefore, it's our responsibility to find ways to also make life fun.

I believe that life philosophy easily presents itself thanks to the concept of Enneagram 7. As of the writing of this book, I am officially standing at the exit door of my very own official midlife crisis. This is the conclusion I have come to:

It's as if I am now qualified to audition for the part of the tortured artist. After all, what's the best we can hope for in this life, if we're being honest? We find ways to cope. That gives us hope or at least distracts us. This is my denial, anger, bargaining, depression, and finally acceptance, of the fact that most of life is monotonous, painful, and out of our control. So, we just keep showing up for the people we love and look for ways to bring meaning, by serving others and enjoying the glimpses of joy we discover along the way.

While that is indeed my original verbiage, the concept goes back thousands of years. It was made famous by King Solomon in the Old Testament book of Ecclesiastes: "So, I commended pleasure, for there is nothing good for a man under the sun except to eat and drink and to be merry, and this will stand by him in his toils throughout the days of his life which God has given him under the sun." (Ecclesiastes 8:15)

The stereotype of an Enneagram 7 is that they focus on always having a good time and/or staying busy so they can outrun their fear of seeing life as empty and meaningless. And that would seem about right for the average Enneagram 7.

However, for a 7 who has matured, I think the healthier view would be more like this:

Life is a gift and time is all we have. The fact that death is a mystery only serves as motivation to make the most of life, by living in the moment with the people who make life meaningful to us.

This reminds me of my favorite quote from what I believe is

one of the most underrated sitcoms of all time: *The Good Place*. In an episode appropriately named "Existential Crisis", the main character Eleanor Shellstrop explains, "You're learning what it is like to be a human. All humans are aware of death. So, we're all a little bit sad, all the time. That's just the deal. And if you try and ignore your sadness, it just ends up leaking out of you anyway. I've been there. And everybody's been there. So don't fight it."

How do we make sense of this paradox that Enneagram 7s remind us of? How do we find a balance of the right amount of happiness in our lives–enough to give life meaning, but not so much happiness that it serves as an unhealthy escape to keep us from working through the tough things in life or that would lead us to a destructive future? I will share with you my answer:

It was by reading the book, *The Happiness Advantage*, that I was able to get a sense of relief that indeed "happiness" is more than just a superficial feeling. Martin Seligman, a pioneer of positive psychology, has broken happiness down into three measurable components: pleasure, engagement, and meaning.

Something my own existential crisis has taught me is that it's ultimately up to me to manage my own happiness. Fortunately, one of the things that helped me climb out of my very own "bottomless pit of despair" was to pull out Maslow's Hierarchy of Needs pyramid that I had remembered learning in college.

Back in 1943, American psychologist Abraham Maslow published "A Theory of Human Motivation" in the journal *Psychological Review*. Here's a thumbnail sketch:

The bottom layer of the pyramid, the Physiological, refers to people who are simply trying to survive by getting their basic needs met: access to clean water and nutritious food, and rest.

The next layer up on the pyramid is Safety: security of their own body from outside harm, as well access to employment, resources, and permanent shelter.

Above that is Love/Belonging: having solid personal relationships with family, friends, and coworkers.

A layer beyond this is Esteem: having a sense of respect, confidence, and achievement.

The final layer that Abraham Maslow describes is Self-Actualization, which focuses on creativity, spontaneity, morality, problem solving, lack of prejudice, and acceptance of facts.

It is my hope that as you are reading this, you can see yourself at the top of Maslow's Hierarchy of Needs pyramid. If so, consider yourself a privileged individual in the course of human history.

One of the reasons I'm attracted to Maslow's theory is that it points out that a person can "have everything," yet still not be happy. It addresses the fact that a man can live in a McMansion with his beautiful wife and honor student children, as he works each day in a very respectable career field, yet he can still have this gnawing fear of missing out and having a feeling of emptiness.

If so, perhaps that man, despite "winning at life", never found his way to the top tier of the pyramid. He never found the time and space for creativity, spontaneity, morality, problem solving, lack of prejudice, and/or acceptance of facts.

I feel that one of the struggles we all face, regardless of our specific Enneagram number, is what I like to call "the illusion of control".

Part of what helped me dig my own way out of my existential crisis, which took several years, was to finally realize that most perceived problems in my life were always out of my control to begin with.

My observation is that modern day tribalism doesn't help this issue. It's easier to believe that the outcome of a sports event or a political election or whether we can convince another person to agree with our own take on whatever the dividing headline is, will somehow affect our individual lives.

I've got some good and bad news rolled into one: None of those distractions actually control our fate. What can control our fate is spending time, energy, and money *believing* they do.

If only we can be more like the Ice Princess Elsa and just "let it go." That has been my experience. I have continued to grow as a person, feeling so much freer by refusing to give power to "fake control" in my life.

I now invite you to join me in the seamless transition to learn about Enneagram 8s, who are next door neighbors to the Self-Driver Variety-Seeker, if they can only recognize that the concept of control is mostly an illusion.

10

TYPE 8: THE SELF-RELIANT CHALLENGER

———————

Main Desire: To be in control and to defend others

Main Fear: To be taken advantage of or be at the mercy of someone else

Go-To Hang-Up: Feeling the need to control everything, feeling betrayed by others

Path to Personal Growth: Accept that you have weaknesses and that being vulnerable about them ironically leads to strength. Acknowledge that you have relational needs that can only be met by others. Realize that sometimes being in control means delegating it to others. Recognize that expressing your emotions can be a gift to others, choosing to see yourself desirable due to your intensity and passion.

"He's MacGyver. He can fix anything. He can build anything. There's nothing he can't figure out!" That has always been an ongoing motto according to my mom, referring to my dad.

She has been saying this for decades, well before I ever heard about the Enneagram. But once I started digging deep into learning the quirks of each type, I realized she was on to something.

As mentioned in the previous chapter on 7s, my dad's own father was in and out of the picture, to the point that my dad ultimately had to become the man of the house. Not only was my dad the father figure to his three younger sisters, but he also financially supported them, along with his mother, while working his way through his teenage years.

It makes me sad to think how he felt shame when he had to make the tough decision to drop out of high school in order to be the provider for his mother and his sister.

That's nothing to be ashamed of. In fact, that is a true example of heroism. An 8's main desire is to be in control and to defend others, which is exactly what he did–he took control and defended others.

Due to his heart of gold, his self-reliant nature, and the skills he taught himself along the way, my dad went on to become one of the most successful, yet humble, men I know in real life.

He never chose to see himself as a victim. Instead, he always found a way to be victorious. While my dad never used words to teach me that lesson, he taught me by example.

When we hear "Enneagram 8," we tend to think of someone like Clint Eastwood, Mark Cuban, or Donald Trump. But I know firsthand, that the majority of 8s in our lives are much more subtle in their tendencies to serve as challengers. My personal favorite example of a famous Enneagram 8 is Martin Luther King, Jr.

Whereas a less mature Enneagram 8 is more inclined to be argumentative and try to prove others wrong, a more mature Enneagram 8 is more focused on proving to themselves that they are capable, despite the odds against them.

The Eight mentality can show up in interesting ways. For my dad, it was in the way he customized his British 1980 MGB, which he impressively upgraded by adding a V8 engine from a Ford Mustang... to make it *American*, of course.

My dad is supposedly a quiet man. It's not something you think about when it's your own dad.

By the time I was a teenager, it was a common occurrence for my friends to discreetly mention to me, "Does your dad *ever* talk?"

I always immediately dismissed it. Of course, my dad talked. He talked all the time! I knew, because I lived with him in the same house.

In fact, he was known as the funniest person in our house! But outside the safety of his home, he became much more reserved.

People were always surprised to learn that my dad competed in martial arts. Still displayed in his bedroom today is his collection of trophies from those years of competitive sparring, including winning 2nd place in the Northeast Alabama region back in 1992.

When I was in 1st grade, my parents decided to become the "den leaders" for the Cub Scouts of my age group.

All throughout my elementary school years, my parents led a dozen of us boys every other Tuesday night in the basement of the First Methodist Church in Fort Payne, Alabama.

My mom handled the administrative aspects of the meetings, while my dad took care of the crafts and badge-earning activities.

Along the way, there were multiple camping trips as well as adventurous hikes.

I will never forget the time my dad was leading us on The Thunderbird Trail in DeSoto State Park when he spotted a deadly rattlesnake ahead.

He picked up the biggest rock he could find and hurled it at the head of the snake, killing it, and making it safe for the rest of us. I would say that sounds like what a Self-Reliant Challenger would do!

Naturally, that snakeskin served as a trophy of awesomeness after that. My friends were so impressed, "I can't believe your dad killed a poisonous snake with his bare hands. That was so cool!"

Let's face it: As a guy, if you could pick your own Enneagram number, I feel like most of us would choose to be an 8.

And similarly, I've noticed that when most married women start to learn about Enneagram, they usually react with, "Oh, I'm sure my husband is an 8!"

I would have to imagine that if as many men were actually 8s who wish they were, and if as many wives were right about their husbands being 8s, the world would have already come to an end. Because that's way too much power in the world!

When I was first diving into the Enneagram, every member of my family and friends quickly endorsed the notion that I am indeed an 8. They weren't completely wrong, as it turns out that's my dominant wing.

In my chapter on Enneagram 6, I mentioned how the Sexual instinct of a 6 resembles an 8. There are other paths to looking like an 8 as well: If you are a 7 or a 9, it is possible your 8 wing can show up a lot in your personality. If you are a 5, you resemble an 8 when you are in growth mode. If you are 2, you resemble an 8 when in stress mode. (Type 2 Ramon just said Amen to that, referring to it as "my warrior coming out.")

Not to mention, the Social instinct of a 2, the Sexual instinct of a 4, and the Self-preservation instincts of a 7 and a 9 can all look like an 8.

It would not be surprising to me if you are growing a little skeptical about the Enneagram at this point, knowing that a 2, 4, 5, 6, 7, and 9 can all be easily confused with an 8, based on our instinct, wing, growth mode, or stress mode.

It may seem easier just to say that everyone is a little bit of all nine types. However, we all have at least a little bit of Enneagram 8 in us.

As the pastor of my church, Derek Bareman, explained to our congregation recently, "We create a coping mechanism during our childhood that compensates for what we are not in order to survive through our teens, our 20s, and our 30s. But by our 40s that same coping mechanism actually begins to hold us back until we confront it."

It is true that even our strengths can ultimately become a weakness when left unchecked over time. I would theorize that Enneagram 8 becomes the coping mechanism for so many of us men, which is not necessarily good for our blood pressure!

Something Enneagram 8s are known for is their desire to leave a mark on this world.

I have this memory of when I was a boy, walking in the woods and seeing this tree with a patch of bark missing, equal to my eye level. I took out a knife, and there I carved these words: "I was here."

Now I am a grown man and that was a lifetime ago, but I'm still always looking for a way to say that same phrase: "I was here."

No one needs to remind me that life is short, so I need to make it count. I am well aware of that!

I'm not a big guy. I don't need to take up much space. I don't need to be the center of attention. I'm good with being brief, being brilliant, and being gone. I just need to find a way to leave my mark.

It just so happens that for me a prime example of an Enneagram 8 happens to be named... you guessed it... *Mark*. In hindsight, I can see that in my vegan phase I was grasping for a sense of control over my life after a failed move to my hometown.

It may sound petty, but I am *always* sizing up every person in the room, to determine who may be a potential foe or ally. One time, at the next table over, I spotted a guy with his family who looked like he was in the same situation as me. His wife probably suggested they all go out for coffee after church.

Before too long, this confident, smiling stranger approached our table. He pointed out that our daughters looked a bit alike and asked how old our little girl was. Within a few minutes, he and I had buddied up at our own table, and he began telling me about how he had founded his own nutrition-based company aimed at helping people meet and maintain their goals on *body recomposition*– or as the rest of us know it– "losing weight" and "getting swole."

Demographically, Mark and I were quite similar. We were even born just a few weeks apart. But one glaring difference is that Mark had the body of a Marvel superhero, and I... had a Stage 1 dad bod.

Mark was specifically drawn to my story. I had spent the majority of my 30s as a vegan, but after turning 35, I could no longer fit into most of my pants.

Despite the plant-based lifestyle being the acclaimed cure-all, as seen on several documentaries streaming on Netflix, I feared being on my way to sharing the same pants size as Zach Galifianakis's character, Alan, in *The Hangover, Part III*: "I'm a 44 slim."

Mark immediately cited the problem and explained it to me: Based on my age, my body had begun producing less testosterone and I was consuming zero "complete protein", which meant I was losing muscle mass and gaining fat mass. Plus based on my daily average calories being so high from vegan junk food my body was storing fuel as fat.

That conversation led to a friendship that was technically based on an ongoing debate between us about whether my vegan lifestyle was sustainable in the long run.

Mark, being the challenger that he is wired to be, successfully became the person who was able to convince me to go back to eating "complete protein" (like eggs, yogurt, fish, and meat) instead of vegan protein (beans, grains, nuts, seeds, fruits, and veggies).

Both my Italian mom and my Italian mother-in-law were so happy the day I announced my conversion back to eating "real food" again.

These days, Mark and I run into each other at the gym quite regularly. He still has the superhero bod. As for me, thanks to him, I was able to get back into my size medium t-shirts and size 31 slim fit pants, which is good enough for me.

One of the things I appreciate most about the way Mark and I communicate is how our conversations are basically an ongoing mutual "diss track".

Spliced in between our dialogue of actual legitimate content, we take turns questioning each other's manhood and overall competence. It's like when you see two dogs who look like they are fighting but are actually just playing.

Thanks to my dominant wing, Enneagram 8 is one of my native languages. I enjoy sparring with an actual Enneagram 8 any chance I get!

Every once in a while, Mark will remind me that despite the way we joke around with each other, he still wants to make sure that "everything is still cool with us". That's what a 9 wing can look like on an Enneagram 8.

I love the way each Enneagram number is balanced out by the numbers next to it. If you are a Self-Confident Challenger, you need your neighbors the Self-Driven Variety-Seeker (7) and the Self-Erasing Negotiator (9) to balance you out.

Another fun example of an Enneagram 8 is my friend Jared. After graduating college, I decided to move to Nashville, and I needed a place to rent. I was fortunate to be introduced to Jared, who had just bought a big house in the wealthiest part of Music City and was looking for roommates.

I know you've seen *Shark Tank* before and are therefore familiar with what a "wantrepreneur" is. Well, that's definitely not Jared. He was the first true entrepreneur I had ever met.

Being just a few years older than me, he had created a business from his home where he somehow made money off people clicking ads on the internet. This story takes place in 2006, by the way, so "SEO" (search engine optimization) was still far from being a household phrase.

There were 5 of us dudes living in that house, including the now famous country music songwriter, Matt Jenkins, who always referred to Jared as "The Godfather." Looking back, now I can see why.

All of us non-entrepreneur roommates were working hard enough to pay the graciously low rent Jared was charging. So nearly every weekend, Jared would take all of us out for dinner at a nice restaurant, encouraging us to order whatever we wanted for our meal.

I remain in touch with Jared and still catch up with him occasionally. When I texted him to let him know I would be using him as an example of an Enneagram 8 in the book I was writing, he simply responded, "*Meh.*"

To me, that's a true sign of an 8. They fundamentally don't care what other people think about them and they do things their own way.

I remember back when we were all roommates, Jared was constantly getting threats for violating the HOA in our neighborhood, whether it was for still having up Christmas lights in April, keeping an arcade cabinet on the front porch, or simply due to all the cars that were always parked on the street in front of his house due to all of us roommates and our visiting friends.

But Jared was never once intimidated. In fact, he was always familiar enough with the local laws that he was able to intimidate the HOA instead. Likewise, when anyone came knocking on his door to try to sell him something or tell him who to vote for in the upcoming election, Jared always immediately shut them down by asking to see their "solicitor permits," which they never had.

A true 8 cannot stand being controlled by others. Jared explained to me that is why he started his own business: He didn't want other people telling him what to do, and for a lot less money than he could figure out how to make it himself.

Jared is a true 8. And yet he is not impressed by his Enneagram number like I am.

Knowing that my dominant wing is an 8, I can look back through my childhood and see how it was always a part of me.

In 5th grade, I decided that instead of playing tag or soccer with the other kids during P.E., I would create and orchestrate a sort of American Gladiators style physical fitness test for everyone to challenge themselves with.

I coordinated this with the gym teacher, gaining approval to utilize all the extra hula hoops, jump ropes, and orange cones. Each day once P.E. began, I set up an obstacle course for each willing participant. With my trusty Casio stopwatch, I was able to determine for sure whether they could complete my course under the time limit I required.

Eventually, word got out on the playground about my program. It even got to the point where I no longer had a reason to recruit; the participants began approaching me, ultimately asking for an invitation.

If you are wondering if I had a name for my physical fitness test, I most certainly did. My dad's nickname for me at the time was Nickbob. Whenever anyone completed my course, I handmade them a customized certificate with their name on it, making it official that they were among the few, the proud, the graduates of... *The Nickbob Ability Test*.

Well, that was fun. We've had a good time learning about what a man actually looks like when he is a true Enneagram 8. If you think that's you, based on what I've covered here, congratulations! You're the number that so many of the rest of us wish we could be.

And if you're not a true 8, and I have just crushed your false reality, well... sorry! No matter what your true number is, the call to action here is to be true to yourself and not try to become someone else you wish you were. As Oscar Wilde said, "Be yourself. Everyone else is already taken." The message of the Enneagram is to discover and understand your unique type and to become the best version, the healthiest version of <u>you</u>.

But if it's any consolation, I want to remind you that as a man, you're likely to flicker in and out of some 8ness throughout the day.

Even if you're not really an 8, there's still a good chance your wife sees you as an Enneagram 8. You can at least hold on to that for now... assuming she's not reading this book before you do.

II

TYPE 9: THE SELF-ERASING NEGOTIATOR

Main Desire: To remain unaffected yet connected

Main Fear: To become separated, to not be at peace

Go-To Hang-Up: Going along with what others do and say, repressing anger due to lack of awareness, denial, or discomfort with the emotion.

Path to Personal Growth: Accept that the world needs you to assert yourself. Acknowledge that your wants and needs matter as much as everyone else's, realizing that keeping the peace with others often does not ensure inner peace if you still feel you are not being heard. Recognize that others want to see you and understand you but that it requires you voicing what you are really thinking, choosing to see yourself as special due to your ability to empathize and harmonize with wisdom that comes natural to you.

Ramon here again. As I said in the chapter about Type 2s, my Nine score is also quite high, so I want to share some thoughts about being a Type 9.

Recently my friend, Mark Nesbitt, told an audience something I relate to as a Type 2 with a lot of attributes of a 9. He said, "When I was a kid there were those U.S. Forest Service ads and TV commercials with Smokey Bear pointing at you and saying, 'Remember only **you** can prevent forest fires.' That's a lot of responsibility and pressure to put on a 6-year-old."

Type 2s and 9s feel a responsibility to prevent disasters if at all possible, and if we can't prevent them then we believe we should be there to help sweep and clean up afterwards.

As I said in the chapter about 2s, my 9ness often competes for the throne. I don't know anyone outside of professional fighters who enjoys conflict, but 9s generally hate conflict. Conflict makes us uncomfortable, nervous, even anxious in anticipation of it, during it, and afterwards. We avoid it if at all possible. We live by the phrase, "I'm a lover, not a fighter."

Being an only child growing up in a single parent home, my house was quiet and peaceful. It was like a library but with a TV or radio on low volume in the background. Plus, my mother and I got along well. Being a cooperative and responsible Type 2, I didn't need much correction or discipline. Bottom line—there wasn't much conflict in our house.

Therefore, I was very uncomfortable at Russ and Brian's house when his mom was yelling at one or both of them. I felt anxious if my friends Mark and Chuck argued. I froze when a coach barked at one of my teammates, or God forbid, at me.

When I think about the level of my discomfort with observing anger or being on the receiving end of it, it's ironic that I'm a couple's therapist. Then again, the peacemaker in me wants to broker peace where and when I can. Professionally, I'm quite adept at staying calm and diffusing volatility, shifting into a voice resembling the late-night DJ of a classical music station. I can do it, but I don't enjoy that part of couple's therapy.

I don't like the moments when I feel like I'm playing referee and should be wearing a black and white striped shirt in the session and holding a whistle in my teeth, ready to blow it and call fouls and penalties. Given my ability to stay calm in a crisis, I would probably make an effective hostage negotiator. Whether in vocation or in hobbies, what we can do is not always what we want to do or what we find fulfillment in doing. Can you relate?

What I'm most unsettled by is someone's anger directed at me. But 9s are not only shaken by someone's anger directed at us; we're also very uncomfortable with our own anger. We're not sure what to do with our anger. And oh, 9s and 2s feel anger, a lot of it actually. You just don't see it in us because we hide it well. Most of the time.

For 9s and 2s, our anger feels like something too hot to hold and too heavy to carry, but we don't know where to set it down. Suppressed briefly, the anger does come out in the warrior who resents feeling bullied or seeks to defend someone else being bullied. I'm a mild-mannered counselor by day, who fantasizes about being an afterhours vigilante bringing justice against villains who have bad mistreated some of my patients.

In my experience, anger generally has two escape routes for

the pressure that builds up. For some 9s, the heat and energy builds and builds until the volcano blows out the top in a brief and furious fit of rage. They explode and then they feel guilt and shame for "losing it."

More often, the vacuum-packed anger slips out through tiny holes in the side of the container via expressions of passive-aggressiveness. Specifically, the passive-aggression is heard in sarcastic and snarky comments and is seen in withdrawing or in withholding behaviors. Withdrawing is shutting down, getting quiet, being less present, less available.

For example, you may become preoccupied with your phone or laptop, or perhaps you regularly retreat to another room to be busy with a project or to watch Netflix. You might present it to your spouse as "I just need some down time," but you know the truth—that you're withdrawing from connection.

What is meant by withholding behaviors is refraining from doing some of the caring gestures you would typically offer to your partner without being asked. For example, you cease making your partner's morning coffee just like they like it. Perhaps you stop offering a kiss goodnight or you "forget" to say goodbye before leaving the house for work. Maybe you stop saying "I love you" or you say it half-heartedly and only if it's said to you first. Withholding behaviors, like most withdrawing actions, are very subtle and yet are intended to be noticed because they are designed to send a message.

The 9's avoidance of conflict and discomfort with anger makes him easy to get along with. In a relationship the 9 is low maintenance because he doesn't ask for much and doesn't complain about much. But it's possible to make being low maintenance too high of a virtue. When you continuously go along to get along, and when you blend in order to be accepted, you not only lose your own voice, you can forget you have one. When that happens, your valid preferences will go unexpressed, your legitimate needs will go unmet, your true feelings will remain unspoken, and your worthy goals and dreams will not raise their hands to be called on.

Then at some point you will resent that. Later in your life, you will have regrets, not so much about what you did do, but about what you didn't do. You will regret not speaking up and will regret not acting. I'm not suggesting you become impulsive, selfish, and offensive. I'm saying that a healthy 9 learns to advocate for himself while also valuing harmony in relationships. The healthy 9 knows he can rock the boat a little bit and the relationship won't sink.

*And now I'm handing the mic back over the Nick to tie this all together:

"I am *not* getting in the pool today. Despite how hot and humid the air is this afternoon, the water is still going to be too cold. I just want to relax. No matter what anybody does or says, I am *definitely not* getting in the pool."

That was the unwavering proclamation I made to my wife on the drive to go hang out with our friends and their kids during the middle of a scorching July Saturday in Tennessee.

As we arrived at the community pool, all the children made their way to the water and the adults assigned themselves to the patio furniture shaded by giant umbrellas.

Our daughter, who was the youngest of the four children there, clearly needed a designated adult to help her be able to swim with the other kids where all the fun was.

My wife turned to me with a smile and kindly asked, "Would you like to go help Holly play in the water?"

You know how this story ends: I spent that afternoon in the pool with all the kids, while the adults hung out in the shade, catching up and enjoying adult beverages.

So basically, I am Paul Rudd.

He is the mascot of what a modern Enneagram 9 guy acts like. In the March 2023 issue of *Men's Health*, he was featured on the cover and gave an interview that helped confirm that I was clearly whatever Enneagram type Paul Rudd happens to be.

"From his earliest roles, Rudd was highly believable when playing frustrated characters, manipulating the anger that resulted from the frustration – and the relief that resulted from overcoming it – for comedic effect."

Whether it's his role as Phoebe's random yet perfectly matched romantic interest in *Friends*, or the newly engaged protagonist of *I Love You, Man* who realizes he has no guy friends to complete a collection of groomsmen for his wedding, or a slightly detached husband and father feeling stuck in life as featured in *This is 40*, Paul Rudd is always the King of Cope.

In writing this chapter, I want to make it clear that the Enneagram number traditionally known as the Peacemaker can look a bit different than the perpetually mellow vibes of Enneagram Nines seen in Mr. Rogers, Bob Ross, Dave Matthews, Jason Mraz, and Bob Marley.

If you're an Enneagram 9 with a dominant 8 wing like me and my buddy Paul Rudd, your anger issues are buried closer to the surface.

Harrison Ford, John Goodman, Woody Harrelson, Brad Pitt, Ryan Gosling, and Liam Neeson are also fellow Nines who are more likely to openly express their frustration and to initiate confrontation and/or conflict, in order to ironically satiate their desire for peace.

I believe a superpower that 9s specifically have is being able to actually make peace *through negotiation*. By naturally serving as a true neutral party and steering the conversation with the self-confidence found in their 8 wing, they have an ability to efficiently lead others to compromise and agreement.

Making peace is more than just by being a "nice person," though one way to easily spot an Enneagram 9 is by their friendliness. I see 9s as the subtle movers and shakers when it comes to discreetly and effortlessly serving as the buffer, effectively de-escalating the tension between people, while not making themselves a target in the drama as the mediator.

Interestingly, Enneagram 9s easily make for ideal "No more Mr. Nice Guy!" characters: Consider John Rambo in *First Blood*, Rocky Balboa in the *Rocky* series, or any character ever played by Jean Claude van Damme.

One of my favorite TV series ever was *The Incredible Hulk*, which ran from 1978 to 1982. I grew up bingeing reruns of that show in the summers. As a boy, I always related to Bruce Banner, portrayed by actor Bill Bixby: "Don't make me angry. You wouldn't like me when I'm angry."

I now realize, in my 40s, there was a reason I always felt connected to the Incredible Hulk. Because like him, I too am an Enneagram 9.

In the chapter on Enneagram 6, I mentioned how some are "Counterphobic 6s", serving as a paradox to the stereotype of an openly fearful and self-doubting 6.

Similarly, there is also what I am naming the "Confrontational

9," serving as a paradox to the stereotype of a passive and conflict-avoidant 9.

I know this because I am the Confrontational 9. I actually get a thrill out of being the person in the group to speak up and say what everyone else is probably thinking. I become energized by any opportunity to call someone out, if their actions appear to be negatively affecting the energy of the group or the environment. I am willing to immediately become assertive, though my default is to remain calm.

Throughout my life, I have been told by others that I can be intimidating, even "scary." I suppose I like that about myself, knowing I have a built-in secret weapon that will prevent me from being too peaceful when the occasion actually calls for mediation initiated by confrontation.

All I ever want is peace. I need inner peace and I need peace in my surroundings. And if I don't obtain the peace I seek, I have this tendency of morphing into my overcompensating 8 wing or my overreaching 1 wing.

I suppose my life matches up to the title of that fourth Superman movie from the 1980s, *The Quest for Peace.*

Now, going back to my name for Enneagram 9s, "The Self-Erasing Negotiator," let's focus a moment on the phrase *self-erasing.*

I could see how for a 9 in a healthier place, the concept of self-erasing can be a very good thing. The more formal way of the phrase is "self-effacing," which according to the APA Dictionary of Psychology, is "to act in such a way as to avoid drawing attention to oneself or making oneself noticeable."

We're familiar with the phrase, "It's not about you."

Out of all the Enneagram types, I would have to imagine that 9s would never need to tape that mantra to their bathroom mirror to serve as a reminder every morning. "It's not about you" is hard-wired into a 9's fundamental operation system. This also implies that for an Enneagram 9 who is in an unhealthy place, they could lean too hard into this concept, and lose their own identity by merging too completely into the people around them.

In case you haven't noticed, I purposely renamed each of the Enneagram types with the word "self." I believe it's important for us to look inward and recognize how we treat ourselves, based on our number.

Here's a rundown of all the types:
1: The Self-Criticizing Reformer
2: The Self-Denying Hidden Warrior
3: The Self-Shaming Achiever
4: The Self-Conscious Innovator
5: The Self-Sufficient Minimalist
6: The Self-Doubting Troubleshooter
7: The Self-Driven Variety Seeker
8: The Self-Reliant Challenger
9: The Self-Erasing Negotiator

As I review all these myself right now, the thing I see that they have in common is that there is an estranged relationship that each Enneagram type has with its own *self*.

In each case, for better *and* for worse, the action of the self serves as the cause, while the effect is the identity being described:

Because 1s are so critical of themselves, they become reformers. Because 2s deny themselves, they become hidden warriors. Because 3s shame themselves, they become achievers. Because 4s are so conscious of themselves, they become innovators. Because

5s are self-sufficient, they become minimalists. Because 6s doubt themselves, they become troubleshooters. Because 7s motivate themselves, they seek variety. Because 8s are self-reliant, they become challengers. And because 9 erase themselves, they become negotiators.

If any Enneagram type deserves the "Chameleon Award," it's the 9s. To know an Enneagram 9 is to know all nine types at all at once, as a result of their instinct to merge with people around them.

In my chapter on Enneagram 3s, I mentioned Tom, my brother-in-law. To help further illustrate what a male Enneagram 9 looks like I'll shine a spotlight on another brother in-law— my younger sister's husband, Andrew.

Having known him for nearly two decades, I can confidently say that Andrew is not the kind of guy who desires a spotlight to be on him. His comfort zone seems to be when he is able to blend in with the crowd.

Think of a person in your life who is always there with you in a crowded room, but who would also be the hardest person to spot in the photo of everyone in that room with you. That just might be the 9 of the group.

However, that doesn't mean that an Enneagram 9 is simply a wallflower. In fact, it's often the 9 who will be first to step up as a mediator to resolve any sense of conflict or confusion, often due to their ability to remove emotion and personal preferences from the equation.

I can honestly say that in knowing Andrew for nearly 20 years, I can't think of a time when he and I ever had a personal disagreement, or even a time when he annoyed me.

The more I understand what triggers my anger and I name those triggers out loud to people close to me, the more I'm able to grow as a person and grow my relationships with others versus withdrawing in repressed anger.

One of the things that fascinates me about the Enneagram, once you figure out which type you are, is to look back throughout your childhood and recall times when your true Enneagram number was on full display.

Every Tuesday morning at my elementary school, my Cub Scout "den" was in charge of placing the American flag on the pole and raising it up for that day.

The flagpole was right there in front of the school where all the parents who were dropping off their kids were able to see such a traditional American event.

Well, one particular Tuesday, some of my fellow Cub Scouts began arguing and scuffling over which one of them would get to be the one to actually pull the rope to raise the flag.

In what was ultimately the 2nd grade version of a fist fight, I was noticeably the only Cub Scout who was not involved in the now infamous "Battle of the Stars and Stripes." The school principal noticed this and rewarded me by assigning me to be in charge of the kid who would officially raise the flag each Tuesday.

A couple years later in 4th grade, my teacher started giving out a "Peacemaker Award" each month, which meant that the selected student won the esteemed privilege of being the line leader for the class. She chose me as the model student for this achievement by making me the first one to receive the award, meaning that the monthly honor probably could have been called "The Nick Shell Award."

(Ramon would like to illustrate his early 9ness by noting that at age 15 he was the recipient of the YMCA Optimist League

Sportsmanship Award for an entire multi-team basketball league. As 9s, we are often very proud of our humbleness.)

Fast forward several years later to my (Nick's) senior year of high school in 1999. The cast of the Senior Play, *Beauty and the Beast*, had just gotten back from going on tour around the elementary schools in town to promote our upcoming performances.

As we arrived back at the high school, all of us were still in costume, the bell had just rung so everyone was walking to their next classes.

It is important to picture me as a 17-year-old guy dressed in a wolf costume, which was no less ridiculous than how the boy Max looked in the classic 1963 children's book, *Where the Wild Things Are*.

Making my way to my next class, I saw a crowd quickly forming aside from the main path. As I neared the frontline, I realized we were just seconds away from two angry female students about to throw their first punches at each other in what would surely be a much more violent fight than the one back in 2nd grade with the Cub Scouts.

I didn't have time to think. I just did what any normal person in a wolf costume would have done in that situation: Throwing my arms up in the air, I began growling and shouting as loud as I could at the two fighters, "*Rrrrroowrrgh! GRRRARRARR! Wowrrroghrrr...*"

Let's just say the theatrical 17-year-old version of me as a wolf was no match for the two high school girls full of rage and spite for one another.

I had won the fight by quickly diffusing it before it could

actually start by making a bigger scene than the two girls or the crowd egging them on.

Try to picture the bizarre state of confusion I placed the fighters in, as they ultimately had no choice but to back away from each other and make their way to class for fear of a deranged mutant wolf possibly attacking them or narcing them out to the first actual adults I saw.

As I walked to my final class that day, I thought to myself, "Did I just randomly and successfully break up a fight by method acting?"

As I have now survived some of the struggles and disappointments that come along with adulthood, I look and feel more like a negotiator than a peacemaker.

How am I a peacemaker in the world now? How am I self-erasing? How do I negotiate?

I think I figured it out. I think I have a solid example for you.

While I have since evolved into a more intense version of my former self, the trade-off is that I have fortunately now recognized the importance of removing myself from the world's game of being tribalistic.

I can contribute to world peace, both globally and locally, as well as my own inner peace, by staying out of the destructive patterns that we are seeing in modern culture: That there are only two perspectives for any topic, and you must therefore choose a side and demonize the other team as wrong, immoral, and/or ignorant, whether it's politics, religion, or even sports!

As a man now in my 40s, I have come to the conclusion that it is a waste of my time and energy to see other people in such an exclusive way.

I get it. Tribalism is a human instinct that guides us to

determine who we deem as safe or a threat. But it seems that the default is now to crank our tribalism levels to full blast and put them on full public display.

It makes me wonder if Enneagram 9s are more inclined to come to this conclusion much earlier in life? That ultimately, being so divisively tribalistic is horrible for inner peace, as well as outer peace.

You can see it in my immediate willingness to accept any person as they are, despite the fact that if I started playing the game of 20 Questions with them, it wouldn't take too long before we both found a personal viewpoint that we didn't see eye to eye on.

Maybe by default, 9s have a bit of a shortcut to accessing emotional intelligence, as they are naturally able to empathize with the other 8 types.

Ultimately, I discovered the Enneagram as the next logical step, after finally realizing that it is always my personal choice to be offended, insulted, or disrespected, even embarrassed or annoyed. I am the one with the set of keys to my own emotions. My perception of reality is often tinted through the lens of my unique personality.

I need to reference Gandhi again here. As an Enneagram 1, he had a 9-wing. So, it's no surprise he stated, "No one can hurt me without my permission."

Therefore, I believe that understanding all nine Enneagram personalities is like walking around with a cheat code for navigating life. I feel like it allows me to hack into the psychological nuances I encounter with every person I communicate with, as well as managing my own anxious thoughts.

Just in case you need to hear this again, of the nine Enneagram types, there is no good one, bad one, best one, worst one. It's not a competition and there are no rankings.

I suppose the only "bad" Enneagram number is any person who discovers their path for growth yet refuses to take steps towards self-improvement. A "good" Enneagram type is any person who discovers their path for growth and starts making the changes necessary in their life to become the best version of their number and themselves.

And from that path to good, you'll also find *better*. You will become the best version of yourself, while accepting that perfection doesn't exist. The closest you can ever get to perfection is through maturing all nine Enneagram types within you, growing into the kind of man this world needs more of:

The Self-Forgiving Reformer; the *Self-Improving* Hidden Warrior; the *Self-Assuring* Achiever; the *Self-Accepting* Innovator; the *Self-Sustaining* Minimalist; the *Self-Trusting* Troubleshooter; the *Self-Balancing* Variety-Seeker; the *Self-Humbling* Challenger; and the *Self-Asserting* Negotiator.

Part III

Deepening Insights About Your Role

12

"WAIT, WHAT'S A WING?" A BRIEF DICTIONARY OF ENNEAGRAM TERMS

Nick and I debated whether to place this chapter here or near the beginning of the book just before the Type chapters. Ultimately, we were concerned that this chapter might overload you with next-level information before you had a chance to grasp the basics.

Regardless, reading this chapter will help you make much more sense out of the next chapter, *Growing Deeper in the Types*.

Ramon: Nick, my intention in creating the baseball diamond & players metaphor was to make the Enneagram seem less mysterious and less complicated right off the bat, no pun intended.

Nick: Right, and we wanted to make the Enneagram more accessible without dumbing it down.

Ramon: Exactly. And the first time I presented this book idea to you I said that I'll be the first to admit that while the Enneagram Baseball Diamond metaphor and image help reduce some of the mysteriousness and complexity of the traditional Enneagram graphic, it has some limitations.

Nick: True. We understood that the tradeoff with the baseball diamond's simplicity is that it cannot illustrate some of the next-level features of the Enneagram (beyond identifying the 9 Types) that the classic Enneagram symbol offers. And those next-level features can be quite insightful and helpful in very practical ways. Okay, so what are you getting at?

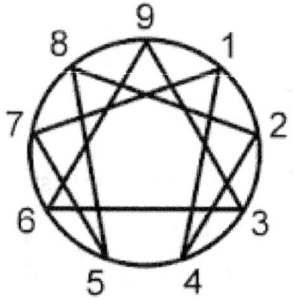

Ramon: Well, we agreed that we would keep our book clear and simple, and that we would provide a Recommended Resources section at the end with plenty of options for readers who wanted to know more about the Enneagram in general and/or more about their own personality.

Nick: Right, and we're still doing that. So...

Ramon: So, I'd like to create a glossary of Enneagram terms and features that the baseball diamond just cannot illustrate. Features that we're not going to explore in depth for every Enneagram personality type. We agree that to do that would be overwhelming for any newcomer to the Enneagram.

Nick: And...

Ramon: And I'd like to include a chapter that explains some of the Enneagram features that guys are likely to hear and wonder about. And by including such a chapter, readers can decide what features interest them and know how to explore those features.

Nick: So, you're saying that the Enneagram is like a Swiss Army Knife that has more tools within it than just the blade. And you want guys to know what the other tools are and how to use them in case they're curious to know more about their Enneagram type and are motivated to make further applications of it in their lives. Is that what you're saying?

Ramon: Ummm, yea. I was actually thinking along the lines of the Russian doll metaphor where there's a doll inside a doll which contains another doll, etc. etc. But I like your Swiss Army Knife metaphor better than a series of hidden ceramics dolls.

Nick: In a book for guys, I'm inclined to go with knives instead of dolls as an analogy.

Ramon: Good point. So, back to the making of a short dictionary of Enneagram terms, what do you think?

Nick: I say, "Go for it."

Ramon: Alright, here we go...

One of the great qualities about the Enneagram is you can splash in the kiddie pool and get plenty of helpful information from even a surface and shallow understanding of just the basics.

If you wish, you can swim in the deeper end of the pool, study more, learn more, understand more, and apply more. And you can do deep ocean dives into the Enneagram for greater depths of insights and applications. Your level of exploration is really up to you. And there is no implied message (or pressure) that you should go deep(er). Let your genuine curiosity and interest be your pacesetter and be your tour guide.

As said above, our Enneagram Baseball Diamond metaphor and image help reduce some of the mysteriousness and complexity of the traditional Enneagram graphic, but it has some limitations. It is not equipped to illustrate some of the advanced features of the Enneagram.

What we want to provide here are some descriptions and explanations of a few additional Enneagram concepts so that if/when you encounter these terms, now and in the future, you can return here to review them.

Your Wings

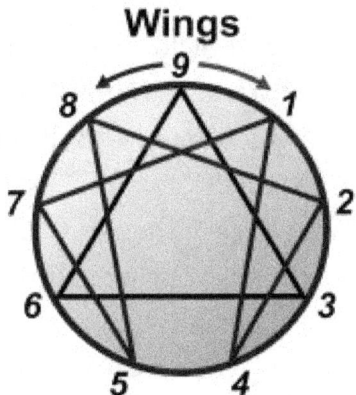

Wings are the most commonly mentioned term along with Enneagram type. Perhaps you've heard someone say, "I'm a 4 wing-5" or "I'm a 3 with a 2-wing." Yea, we know; it's weird. It sounds like it could be a secret code for a psychological abnormality.

"Yea, my psychiatrist diagnosed me and said I'm a 7 wing-6, and he put me on a new medication. I no longer talk to phone poles, but now my hair hurts."

Identifying your wings is rather straightforward. In looking at the traditional Enneagram graphic, you see that for any single number there is another number on each side. The two numbers are the two potential Wings of your Enneagram type.

Since no one is a pure personality type, everyone is a unique mixture of his basic type and usually *one* of the two types adjacent to it. This is why you'll hear someone refer to themselves as a "2 wing-1" and not a "2 wing-1 & 3."

Saying "I'm a 2 with a 1 wing and a 3 wing" would be like saying "I play centerfield which is in the middle between left field and right."

Everyone knows that centerfield is between left and right field.

But if I said, "I play centerfield, but I move a few steps toward right field when there's a left-handed pull hitter," that tells you something that's not obvious.

For example, the two wings of the 9 are 8 & 1.

Your basic type dominates your overall personality, while the wing complements it and adds important, sometimes contradictory, elements to your total personality. Your wing is the "second side" of your personality, and it must be taken into consideration to better understand yourself or someone else.

For example, if you are a type Nine, you will likely have either a One-wing or an Eight-wing, and your personality as a whole can best be understood by considering the traits of the Nine as they uniquely blend with the traits of either the One or the Eight.

So, how do I know what my dominant Wing is?

At the risk of this sounding oversimplified, read the descriptions in this book about both your wing types and discern which wing sounds more like you.

So, for example, if you're a type Nine, read through the main characteristics of Enneagram Ones and Eights and discern whether you resemble more of a standard One or a typical Eight. (By the way, identify and select the wing that best describes you, and not the wing you think you should be or that you wish you were.)

Your Arrows

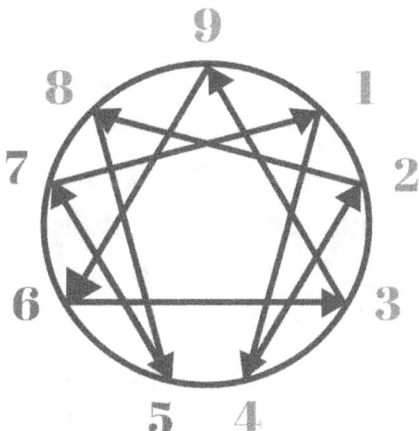

You might have to be as old as me to recall the 1970 Henry Nilsson love song "Me and My Arrow" with lyrics such as

> *Me and my Arrow*
> *Straighter than narrow*
> *Wherever we go*
> *Everyone knows*
> *It's me and my Arrow.*

You gotta feel some sympathy for a girl whose parents named her "Arrow." It also makes you wonder if perhaps they named their son "Beau." But I digress...

You're unlikely to write a song about your Enneagram arrows, and unlike Nilsson, you have two arrows instead of just one.

What do the arrows mean?

There are two types of arrows that branch to and from your Enneagram type, indicating where you tend to go in Security and in Stress.

The line extending away from your Enneagram number (follow the away arrow) indicates your unhealthy side number or the type you are inclined to go to in stress, under pressure, and in conflict.

The line coming into your Enneagram number (the arrow comes to you) indicates your healthiest side number or the type you are inclined to go to when you're operating from a healthy and secure version of your type.

For example, let's say you're a 5. When you're operating as an immature 5 and under stress, you can take on the negative characteristics of an unhealthy 7. You can become superficial, aimless, restlessly seeking diversions.

On the other hand, when you're operating as a mature 5 and feeling secure you can take on the best characteristics of a healthy 8. You're more apt to convert your knowledge into action, confidently making positive changes in the world in bolder ways.

Your Center (or Triad)

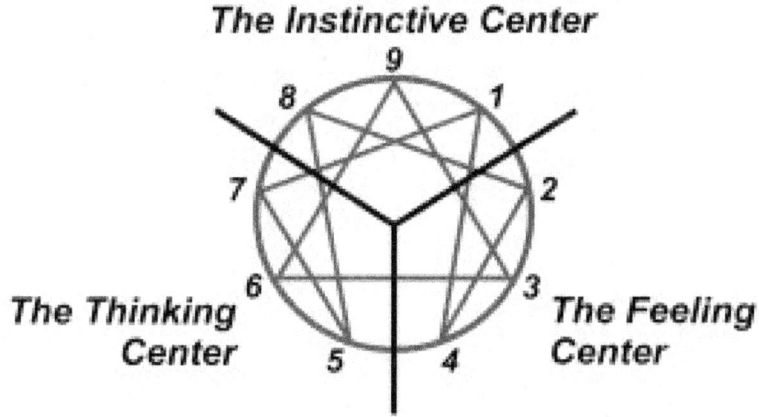

These three centers (or triads) are often referred to as the Centers of Intelligence which is an unfortunate and potentially misleading name because these three centers have nothing to do with your level of intelligence. (Besides, we believe that your interest in our book clearly confirms that you are extremely intelligent.)

What your Center refers to is your natural way of processing information from your environment and experiences.

The Enneagram is a 3 x 3 arrangement of nine personality types in *three Centers*. There are three types in the *Body Center*, three in the *Heart Center*, and three in the *Head Center*, as shown below. These are also known as the *Action or Instinctive Center*, the *Feeling Center*, and the *Thinking Center*. Each Center consists of three personality types that have in common the assets and liabilities of that Center.

For example, if you're a 3 you have unique strengths and liabilities involving your feelings, which is why it is in the Heart Center. If you're a 5 you're located in the Head Center because your strengths and your struggles are likely to involve your thoughts. If you're an 8, your assets and liabilities will lie in the Instinctive or Body Center because you are naturally action oriented.

Your Instinct

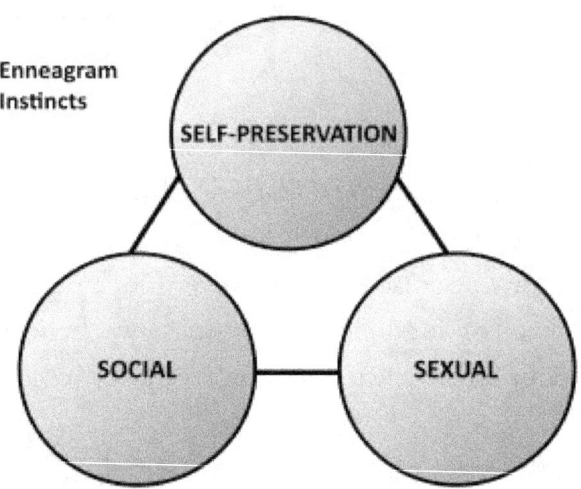

The three Instincts are another set of distinctions that are useful in understanding your personality. A major aspect of human nature lies in our instinctual "hard wiring" as biological beings. We each are endowed with specific instincts that are necessary for our survival as individuals and as a species. We each have a *Self-preservation* instinct (for preserving the body and its life and functioning), a *Sexual* instinct (for extending ourselves in the environment and through the generations), and a *Social* instinct (for getting along with others and forming secure social bonds).

While we have all three Instincts in us, one of them is the dominant focus of our attention and behavior—the set of attitudes and values that we are most attracted to and comfortable with. We each also have a second Instinct that is used to support the dominant Instinct, as well as a third Instinct that is the least developed—a real blind spot in our personality and our values. Which Instinct is in each of these three places—most, middle, and least developed—produces what we call our "Instinctual Stack" (like a three-layer cake) with your dominant instinct on top, the next most developed instinct in the middle, and the least developed on the bottom.

These instinctual drives profoundly influence our personalities, and at the same time, our personalities largely determine how each person *prioritizes* these instinctual needs. Thus, while every human being has all three of these instincts operating in him or her, our personality causes us to be more concerned with one of these instincts than the other two. We call this instinct our *dominant* instinct. This tends to be our first priority—the area of life we attend to first.

Further, our Enneagram type flavors the way in which we approach our dominant instinctual need. Combining our Enneagram type with our dominant instinct yields a much more specific portrait of the workings of our personality. When we apply the distinctions of these three instincts to the nine

Enneagram types, they create 27 unique combinations of type and dominant instinct that account for differences and variability within the types. These combinations are called the Instinctual Variants or Subtypes. More about subtypes in a moment. But first, let's focus on Instincts.

The following are brief descriptions of the three Instincts:

Self-Preservation Instinct

People who have this as their dominant instinct are preoccupied with safety, comfort, health, energy, and well-being. In a word, they are concerned with having enough *resources* to meet life's demands.

One of those resources is financial. Therefore, a person with the self-preservation instinct is likely to have a different definition and measurement of "financial security" than a person with one of the other instincts.

Do you see how your Enneagram Type (and your Wing, and your Instinct) can influence your attitude about money? You may *believe* that you've simply *chosen* your level of risk tolerance for investing because of the research you've done on the history and trends of the stock market, but that's not it. Now, it's not that your research and conclusions are irrelevant, but your personality so profoundly influences your relationship with money that your personality influences how you interpret the economic data, not the other way around. Your personality will tend to look to the data to confirm your natural risk tolerance.

We may think we make "totally objective" decisions, but we don't...because it's impossible to do so. We hopefully make "well-informed" decisions, but we are incapable of making choices and decisions from a place of absolute objectivity, because our personality, preferences, emotions, and biases are always riding with us on the bus, if not driving it.

Self-Preservation types tend to be more grounded, practical, serious, and introverted than the other two instinctual types. They might have active social lives and a satisfying intimate relationship, but if they feel that their self-preservation needs are not being met, they tend to be unhappy or less at ease. In their primary relationships they seek domestic tranquility and security with a stable, reliable partner.

Sexual (aka "Attraction") Instinct

The Sexual instinct is unfortunately named because the phrase can be misleading, so keep reading. Many people originally identify themselves as this type because they have learned that the Sexual types are interested in "one-on-one relationships." But all three instinctual types are interested in one-on-one relationships, just for different reasons, so this does not necessarily distinguish them. The Sexual type, however, is likely to be *more* interested in and responsive to 1:1 relationships.

The key element in Sexual types is an intense drive for stimulation and a constant awareness of the "chemistry" between themselves and others. Sexual types are immediately aware of the attraction, or lack thereof, between themselves and other people. There are many people we are excited to be around for reasons of personal chemistry who we have no sexual attraction to or romantic feelings for. Nonetheless, we might be aware that we feel stimulated or energized in certain people's company and less so in others.

You're likely reading this and thinking, "Well, duh! Yea, I like some people more than others. But that's true for everybody."

And yes, that generalization is absolutely true. We all like some people more than others. Frankly, some people are generally more likeable than others. Some fall into the EGR category—Extra Grace Required.

You can probably think of someone in your immediate or extended family or someone you've worked with that everyone seems to love and enjoy being around. And you can think of someone in your family or social network that people just tolerate and avoid if possible.

First off, kind people are more likeable, period. Undoubtedly, you've seen the bumper sticker that reads, "Mean people suck!" I have said regarding being in close relationship with any chronically negative and critical person, "It's hard to want to hug a porcupine."

Beyond general kindness, we will be drawn to those whose personality we like and with whom we have things in common. And yes, that sounds like "compatibility," because it is exactly that.

But for the Sexual type, chemistry is much more than just compatibility. "There's a certain *je ne sais quoi*," we might say when we like something or someone and can't find just the right words to explain the attraction or affection.

Again, we all experience that to a degree, but the feeling is more significant and more sought after for the Sexual type. Sexual types tend to be constantly moving toward that sense of intense stimulation and energy in their relationships and in their activities. They are the most "energized" of the three instinctual types, and tend to be more aggressive, competitive, charged, and emotionally intense than the Self-Preservation or Social types.

Those with the Sexual instinct need to have an intense

energetic charge in their primary relationships or else they remain unsatisfied or become bored. They enjoy being intensely involved—even merged—with others and can become disenchanted with partners who are unable to meet their need for intense energetic union. This can mean that some Sexual types are not averse to creating some drama or even stirring up conflict to liven things up in a relationship. Whereas the Self-Preservationist is concerned about losing security and stability in a relationship, those with the Sexual instinct are wary of stagnation and boredom.

Social (aka "Adaptive") Instinct

Just as many people tend to misidentify themselves as Sexual types because they want one-on-one relationships, many people fail to recognize themselves as Social types because they get the (false) idea that this means always being involved in groups, meetings, and parties. If Self-Preservation types are interested in adjusting the environment to make themselves more secure and comfortable, Social types *adapt themselves to serve the needs of the social situation* they find themselves in.

Thus, Social types are highly aware of other people, whether they are in intimate situations or in groups. They are also aware of how their actions and attitudes are affecting those around them. Moreover, while Sexual types seek intimacy, Social types seek *personal connection*. They want to stay in long-term contact with people and to be involved in their world.

Social types are the most concerned with doing things that will have some impact on their community or on even broader domains. They tend to be warmer, more open, engaging, and socially responsible than the other two types.

In their primary relationships, they seek partners with whom they can share social activities, wanting their intimates to get involved in projects and events with them. Paradoxically, they actually tend to avoid long periods of exclusive intimacy and quiet solitude, seeing both as potentially limiting. Social types can lose their sense of identity and meaning when they are not involved with others in activities that transcend their individual interests.

Your Subtype

I've heard that there are 27 possible Enneagram subtypes? 27?! Seriously? Gimme a break.

Yes, but relax; you can narrow your subtype down to just three options. The formula to identify your subtype is simply

Your Main Type or Number + Your Dominant Instinct = Your Subtype

So, for example, if you're a Type 7, you may be a Social 7, a Sexual 7, or a Self-Preservation 7.

I've been hesitant to mention and list the subtypes in the book for fear of giving you information overload and provoking the feeling that you are trying to sip water from a firehose. But as I said earlier, Nick and I want to offer and explain some terms you may encounter and wonder what they mean. Secondly, if you'll forgive the repetition of an earlier comment, the Enneagram allows you swim on the surface for valuable and applicable insights and it invites you to go deeper if you wish for more detailed and specific analysis and application.

As one who has snorkeled in the Bahamas and scuba dived

in south Florida, I can tell you there is a lot of amazing coral reefs and colorful fish you can enjoy by floating on the surface in shallow water if you're in the right place. But there are just some things you will not see and experience without donning scuba gear and diving down to explore a world that only exists 60—90 feet beneath the surface of the ocean. Again, I've done both, and both are exhilarating. Take your pick or do both. I will say that as a progression I snorkeled in open water before I ever put on a scuba tank. Likewise, as you get into the waters of the Enneagram, we recommend that you just enjoy surface swimming and snorkeling for a while if/before you also choose to do a deeper dive.

Okay, without further ado, here are the 27 Subtypes. Simply find your main type/number, review the three options, and discern which one sounds the *most* like you. It's likely you're going to see yourself in all three subtypes listed there because they are all within your main personality type. You will likely express all three instincts of your type from time to time as influenced by the situation you're in. But your true subtype will be the one that best describes you or that describes you most of the time. (We *want to give credit to and thank Evan Doyle at EnneagramGift.com for his assistance with describing the 27 subtypes.*)

Type 1 Subtypes

Self-Preservation 1s: **The Safety-Seeking Pioneer**
Focuses on creating a safe and structured environment, pioneering efficient ways to ensure security.

Social 1s: **The Communal Crusader**
Feels responsible for improving the community, challenging and refining societal norms.

Sexual 1s: **The Idealistic Advocate**

Passionately promotes personal principles, expecting others to uphold these standards.

Type 2 Subtypes
Self-Preservation 2s: The Caring Custodian
Derives self-worth from caring for close ones, seeing it as their duty.
Sexual 2s: The Passionate Charmer
Forms deep connections using charm, drawing others closer
Social 2s: The Networked Diplomat
Acts as a connector or diplomat within broader social networks.

Type 3 Subtypes
Self-Preservation 3s: The Corporate Climber
Strives for security in structured environments, seeking visible rewards and recognition.
Sexual 3s: The Alluring Icon
Emphasizes allure and charm, captivating others with magnetism
Social 3s: The Image-Conscious Influencer
Values societal acknowledgment, ensuring a polished public image.

Type 4 Subtypes
Self-Preservation 4s: The Artistic Maverick
Uses creativity to shield from external threats, celebrating their unique identity.
Sexual 4s: The Soulful Competitor
Seeks depth in relationships, often with a dramatic or competitive flair.
Social 4s: The Authenticity Advocate

Struggles with societal norms, oscillating between shame and the pride of authenticity.

Type 5 Subtypes
Self-Preservation 5s: **The Fortress Mind**
Considers personal space a refuge, fortifying with knowledge and introspection.

Sexual 5s: **The Enigmatic Confidant**
Forms bonds over shared secrets or specialized knowledge, maintaining an air of mystery.

Social 5s: **The Conceptual Scholar**
Engages socially through shared concepts, ideas, or knowledge.

Type 6 Subtypes
Self-Preservation 6s: **The Comfort Guardian**
Finds solace in predictable relationships, especially family bonds.

Sexual 6s: **The Protective Partner**
Values strength and security in personal relationships.

Social 6s: **The Civic Defender**
Upholds community values, often safeguarding societal norms.

Type 7 Subtypes
Self-Preservation 7s: **The Sensory Connoisseur**
Savors life's experiences, seeking varied pleasures and delights.

Sexual 7s: **The Curious Explorer**
Drawn to new experiences and relationships, captivated by fascination.

Social 7s: **The Visionary Dreamer**
Chases idealistic visions of society, often with personal sacrifices.

Type 8 Subtypes

Self-Preservation 8s: **The Resilient Maverick**

Stands independent, thriving in challenges and asserting dominance.

Sexual 8s: **The Intense Devotee**

Engages in relationships with deep intensity, either dominating or surrendering fully.

Social 8s: **The Cause Champion**

Leads and fights for social causes or justice, demanding respect.

Type 9 Subtypes

Self-Preservation 9s: **The Serene Collector**

Finds comfort in collecting or savoring memories and experiences.

Sexual 9s: **The Unifying Partner**

Seeks deep unity in relationships, blending their identity with their partner's.

Social 9s: **The Harmonious Contributor**

Participates in communities, often as a peacekeeper or helper.

Remember there is no better or worse subtype just as there is not a better or worse main Type. Just like every main Enneagram type has potential strengths and weaknesses, the same is true with subtypes. And as with the main Enneagram types, you are not all of just one subtype with no attributes of the other two. You're a blend, but it's helpful to identify your dominant type, your dominant subtype, and your dominant time orientation.

Wait, what? My dominant time orientation? What's that?

I'm glad you asked.

Your Time Orientation

Time orientation is where we focus most of our thoughts and attention.

Since we have access to all three orientations, if you're a Past Oriented person, consciously choosing to experience the present moment or planning for future goals would be healthy, holistic practices to engage in.

If you're a Future Oriented guy, you'll benefit from being intentional about being more present in the moment, and you'll profit from reflecting on the past–what went well or wrong, and what you can learn from those experiences.

If you're Present Oriented, then past and future thinking can help move you forward when you're stuck and ruminating in the moment. The key in engaging your time orientation is to accept and embrace how your time orientation has helped you to survive and to succeed, while also recognizing when the opportunity or need calls for a shift to a different time orientation.

Let's look at your Enneagram Type in the context of your Time Orientation

Past Orientation: Types 4, 5, and 9

Type Four: Four's thoughts and emotions center most often on what has already happened, what they regret, or an ideal experience they romanticize.

Type Five: Five's thoughts center most often on analyzing what has already happened, making sense of previous experiences and feelings, and coming up with logical solutions to earlier problems.

Type Nine: Nines ruminate about how their lives were both positive and negative in the past, feeling stuck and unable to alter negative patterns or improve the good ones.

Present Orientation: Types 1, 2, and 6

Type One: Ones act in either a flurry of movement or methodical steps, to correct and perfect moment-by-moment the things that come to their attention.

Type Two: Type Two's thoughts and emotions center often on what someone else needs, seeking to fulfill it immediately, without regard to past experiences or future consequences.

Type Six: Sixes immerse themselves in whatever current situation is triggering their danger warning system.

Future Orientation: Types 3, 7, and 8

Type Three: Threes are planning how to efficiently complete the next task and thinking about ways to successfully achieve their goals.

Type Seven: Sevens can be constantly in motion, thinking about what next fun thing to do and moving toward an ever-evolving horizon.

Type Eight: Eights seek to pave the way toward their goals by planning exactly how to power past any and all obstacles.

Okay, Take a Deep Breath

See, we told you—you can explore various depths of your personality via the Enneagram. How close to the surface you swim or how deep you dive is completely up to you. The most experienced teachers of the Enneagram recommend starting and sticking with the basics for a while until you feel you have a good working understanding of your main number and are making helpful applications in your life and relationships from that core knowledge. Then if/when you're interested and ready, you can explore and discover insights about your wings or your instinct or your subtype or your time orientation.

At the end of this book, you'll find a recommended resources section with many ways to learn more.

13

GOING DEEPER IN THE TYPES

Here at a glance, you can view the advanced features of your Type as described in the previous chapter.

Type 1: The Self-Criticizing Reformer

Wings
Type 9: The Self-Erasing Negotiator
Type 2: The Self-Denying Hidden Warrior

Arrows
In stress mode, 1 resembles an unhealthy 4.
In growth mode, 1 resembles a healthy 7.

Center or Triad

Type 1s reside in the Body Triad. The common emotion is anger. Type Ones take in and process information based more on feelings than facts, while struggling for things to be made right, as they also seek to discern what action to take. Type 1s tend to internalize anger, while 9s ignore it and 8s outwardly express it.

Subtypes

Self-Preservation 1s: **The Safety-Seeking Pioneer**
Focuses on creating a safe and structured environment, pioneering efficient ways to ensure security.

Social 1s: **The Communal Crusader**
Feels responsible for improving the community, challenging and refining societal norms.

Sexual 1s: **The Idealistic Advocate**
Passionately promotes personal principles, expecting others to uphold these standards.

Time Orientation

Present: Ones tend to act in either a flurry of movement or methodical steps, to correct and perfect moment-by-moment the things that come to their attention. Because Ones are instinctively inclined to focus on the present and what/who is in front of them, their growth challenge will be to look up and look backwards and ahead, being mindful of reviewing the past and being intentional about future planning.

Negative Thinking Traps

All or Nothing: You look at things in absolute, black-and-white categories. There are only victories and defeats. The glass is either completely full or it's empty.

Should Statements: You mercilessly criticize yourself with "I should..." or "I should have...", "I never should have..." Should statements also work against other people to fuel your resentment.

Labeling: You identify yourself by your shortcomings. Instead of saying, "I made a mistake," you tell yourself, "I'm a failure," "I'm a fool," "I'm so stupid," "I'm an idiot, or "I am a loser." You are inclined to label others as well.

Type 2: The Self-Denying Hidden Warrior

Wings
Type 1: The Self-Criticizing Reformer
Type 3: The Self-Shaming Achiever

Arrows
In stress mode, 2 resembles an unhealthy 8.
In growth mode, 2 resembles a healthy 4.

Center or Triad
A man who is a Type 2 will likely reside in the Heart Triad. His common emotion is shame. He takes in information through his emotional centers, while struggling with the insecurity that he is good enough. The Two may attempt to address and sooth his shame by trying to win the affection of others, while 3s try to earn others' admiration, and 4s try to embody enough uniqueness and individuality to prove their worth to themselves.

Subtypes

Self-Preservation 2s: **The Caring Custodian**

Derives self-worth from caring for close ones, seeing it as their duty.

Sexual 2s: **The Passionate Charmer**

Forms deep connections using charm, drawing others closer

Social 2s: **The Networked Diplomat**

Acts as a connector or diplomat within broader social networks.

Time Orientation

Present: Type Two's emotions and thoughts center often on what someone else needs, seeking to fulfill it immediately, without regard to past experiences or future consequences. Because Twos are instinctively inclined to focus on the present and what/who is in front of them, their growth challenge will be to look up and look backwards and ahead, being mindful of reviewing the past and being intentional about future planning.

Negative Thinking Traps

Personalization: You completely blame yourself for something you weren't entirely responsible for. Or you blame other people and overlook ways that your own attitudes or actions might have contributed to the problem.

Mental Filter: You dwell on the negatives and ignore the positives. It's like the way that one drop of food coloring in a large glass of water changes the color of the entire volume of water. Some are inclined to focus on the positives and ignore or deny any negatives.

Mind Reading: You assume that people are reacting negatively to you when in fact you have no definitive evidence for this. We give ourselves enormous credit for being able to rightly guess someone's thoughts, feelings, attitudes, reasons, and intentions.

Type 3: The Self-Shaming Achiever

Wings
Type 2: The Self-Denying Hidden Warrior
Type 4: The Self-Conscious Innovator

Arrows
In stress mode, 3 resembles an unhealthy 9.
In growth mode, 3 resembles a healthy 6.

Center or Triad
For the guy who is a Type 3 he will most often work out of the Heart Triad. His common emotion is shame. He takes in information through his emotional center while struggling with the insecurity that he is adequate. Type 3s will seek to address their shame by trying to earn others' admiration, while 2s try to win the affection of others, and 4s try to embody enough uniqueness and individuality to prove their worth to themselves.

Subtypes
Self-Preservation 3s: **The Corporate Climber**
Strives for security in structured environments, seeking visible rewards and recognition.
Sexual 3s: **The Alluring Icon**
Emphasizes allure and charm, captivating others with magnetism
Social 3s: **The Image-Conscious Influencer**

Values societal acknowledgment, ensuring a polished public image.

Time Orientation

Future: Threes are planning how to efficiently complete the next task and are thinking about ways to successfully achieve their goals. In their natural future orientation, the Three's growth challenge is being mindful and intentional about being more present in the moment, and choosing to reflect on the past–what went well or wrong, and what can be learned from those experiences. Reminder: Success leaves clues and we can learn from our mistakes.

Negative Thinking Traps

Disqualifying the Positive: You insist that your accomplishments or positive qualities don't count. This may seem similar to Mental Filter. The difference is that Mental Filter dwells upon and is stuck on the negative. DtP ignores or dismisses the positives as irrelevant.

Minimization: This is also called the "binocular trick." Looking through the wrong end of your emotional binoculars you shrink your positive qualities or abilities almost to insignificance.

Should Statements: You mercilessly criticize yourself with "I should..." or "I should have...", "I never should have..." Should statements also work against other people to fuel your resentment.

Type 4: The Self-Conscious Innovator

Wings
Type 3: The Self-Shaming Achiever
Type 5: The Self-Sufficient Minimalist

Arrows
In stress mode, 4 resembles an unhealthy 2.
In growth mode, 4 resembles a healthy 1.

Center or Triad
The Type 4 resides in the Heart Triad. The common emotion is shame. He takes in and processes information through his emotional centers while struggling with the insecurity that he is good enough, often feeling that he is different and doesn't quite fit in. Type 4s address their shame by trying to embody enough uniqueness and individuality to prove their worth to themselves, while 3s try to earn others' admiration, and 2s try to win the affection of others.

Subtypes
Self-Preservation 4s: **The Artistic Maverick**
Uses creativity to shield from external threats, celebrating their unique identity.
Sexual 4s: **The Soulful Competitor**
Seeks depth in relationships, often with a dramatic or competitive flair.
Social 4s: **The Authenticity Advocate**

Struggles with societal norms, oscillating between shame and the pride of authenticity.

Time Orientation

Past: Four's emotions and thoughts center most often on what has already happened, what they regret, or an ideal experience they romanticize. Since a Four instinctively leans toward a past orientation, the growth challenge is being mindful and intentional in choosing to experience the present moment and to plan for future goals and needs.

Negative Thinking Traps

Emotional Reasoning: You give too much authority, too much credit to your feelings as a reliable informant on reality. This can be summarized as "I feel it therefore it is true."

Catastrophizing: You believe the worst-case scenario is the most likely outcome.

Mind Reading: You assume that people are reacting negatively to you when in fact you have no definitive evidence for this. We give ourselves enormous credit for being able to rightly guess someone's thoughts, feelings, attitudes, reasons, and intentions.

Type 5: The Self-Sufficient Minimalist

Wings

Type 4: The Self-Conscious Innovator
Type 6: The Self-Doubting Troubleshooter

Arrows

In stress mode, 5 resembles an unhealthy 7.

In growth mode, 5 resembles a healthy 8.

Center or Triad

Type 5s tend to operate in the Head Triad. Their common emotion is fear. They take in information analytically through their mind, while struggling with making decisions and planning for the future. Fives are prone to retreat inward, fearing they cannot navigate the outside world, while 6s move outward towards sources of security and guidance, and 7s move towards what they believe will lead them to satisfaction, as well as distraction from pain or boredom.

Subtypes

Self-Preservation 5s: **The Fortress Mind**
Considers personal space a refuge, fortifying with knowledge and introspection.
Sexual 5s: **The Enigmatic Confidant**
Forms bonds over shared secrets or specialized knowledge, maintaining an air of mystery.
Social 5s: **The Conceptual Scholar**
Engages socially through shared concepts, ideas, or knowledge.

Time Orientation

Past: Five's thoughts center most often on analyzing what has already happened, making sense of previous experiences and feelings, and coming up with logical solutions to earlier problems. Since a Five instinctively leans toward a past orientation, the growth challenge is being mindful and intentional in choosing to experience the present moment and to plan for future goals and needs.

Negative Thinking Traps

All or Nothing: You look at things in absolute, black-and-white categories. There are only victories and defeats. The glass is either completely full or it's empty.

Labeling: You identify yourself by your shortcomings. Instead of saying, "I made a mistake," you tell yourself, "I'm a failure," "I'm a fool," "I'm so stupid," "I'm an idiot, or "I am a loser." You are inclined to label others as well.

Fortune Telling: You instinctively predict that things will turn out badly. Your crystal ball seems to only project negative outcomes.

Type 6: The Self-Doubting Troubleshooter

Wings
Type 5: The Self-Sufficient Minimalist
Type 7: The Self-Driven Variety Seeker

Arrows
In stress mode, 6 resembles an unhealthy 3.
In growth mode, 6 resembles a healthy 9.

Center or Triad
Type 6 males function in the Head Triad. The common emotion is fear. They take in and processes information analytically through their mind while struggling with making decisions and planning for the future. Sixes move outward towards sources of security and guidance, while 7s move towards what they believe will lead them to satisfaction, as well as

distraction from pain or boredom; and 5s retreat inward, fearing they cannot navigate the outside world.

Subtypes

Self-Preservation 6s: **The Comfort Guardian**
Finds solace in predictable relationships, especially family bonds.

Sexual 6s: **The Protective Partner**
Values strength and security in personal relationships.

Social 6s: **The Civic Defender**
Upholds community values, often safeguarding societal norms.

Time Orientation

Present: Sixes immerse themselves in whatever current situation is triggering their danger warning system. Because Sixes are instinctively inclined to focus on their immediate concerns or worries, their growth challenge will be to look up and look backwards and ahead, being mindful of beneficially reviewing the past and being intentional about planning for future goals and needs.

Negative Thinking Traps

Disqualifying the Positive: You insist that your accomplishments or positive qualities don't count. This may seem similar to Mental Filter. The difference is that Mental Filter dwells upon and is stuck on the negative. DtP ignores or dismisses the positives as irrelevant.

Catastrophizing: You believe the worst-case scenario is the most likely outcome.

Overgeneralization: You view a negative event as a never-ending pattern of defeat. The clue here is the prevalent use of "always" and "never" in your language. Also watch for the negative use of these absolute words: every, all, none, everything, nothing, anything, anyone, everyone, nobody.

Type 7: The Self-Driven Variety Seeker

Wings
Type 6: The Self-Doubting Troubleshooter
Type 8: The Self-Reliant Challenger

Arrows
In stress mode, 7 resembles an unhealthy 1.
In growth mode, 7 resembles a healthy 5.

Center or Triad
Type Sevens are located in the Head Triad. The common emotion is fear. Sevens take in information analytically through their minds while struggling with making decisions and planning for the future. Sevens move toward what they believe will lead them to satisfaction, as well as to distraction from pain or boredom; while 6s move outward towards sources of security and guidance, and 5s retreat inward, fearing they cannot navigate the outside world.

Subtypes
Self-Preservation 7s: **The Sensory Connoisseur**
Savors life's experiences, seeking varied pleasures and delights.
Sexual 7s: **The Curious Explorer**
Drawn to new experiences and relationships, captivated by fascination.

Social 7s: The Visionary Dreamer
Chases idealistic visions of society, often with personal sacrifices.

Time Orientation

Future: Sevens can be constantly in motion, thinking about what next fun thing to do and moving toward an ever-evolving horizon. In their natural future orientation, the Seven's growth challenge is being mindful and intentional about being more present in the moment, and choosing to reflect on the past–what went well or wrong, and what can be learned from those experiences. Reminder: Success leaves clues and we can learn from our mistakes.

Negative Thinking Traps

Disqualifying the Positive: You insist that your accomplishments or positive qualities don't count. This may seem similar to Mental Filter. The difference is that Mental Filter dwells upon and is stuck on the negative. DtP ignores or dismisses the positives as irrelevant.

Catastrophizing: You believe the worst-case scenario is the most likely outcome.

Overgeneralization: You view a negative event as a never-ending pattern of defeat. The clue here is the prevalent use of "always" and "never" in your language. Also watch for the negative use of these absolute words: every, all, none, everything, nothing, anything, anyone, everyone, nobody.

Type 8: The Self-Reliant Challenger

Wings
Type 7: The Self-Driven Variety Seeker
Type 9: The Self-Erasing Negotiator

Arrows
In stress mode, 8 resembles an unhealthy 5.
In growth mode, 8 resembles a healthy 2.

Center or Triad
The Type 8 guy functions in the Body Triad. His common emotion is anger. He takes in information based on instincts rather than facts, while struggling for things to be made right. The Eight outwardly expresses anger, whereas Nines ignore it, and Ones internalize it.

Subtypes
Self-Preservation 8s: **The Resilient Maverick**
Stands independent, thriving in challenges and asserting dominance.
Sexual 8s: **The Intense Devotee**
Engages in relationships with deep intensity, either dominating or surrendering fully.
Social 8s: **The Cause Champion**
Leads and fights for social causes or justice, demanding respect.

Time Orientation

Future: Eights seek to pave the way toward their goals by planning exactly how to power past any and all obstacles. In their natural future orientation, the Eight's growth challenge is being mindful and intentional about being more present in the moment, and choosing to reflect on the past–what went well or wrong, and what can be learned from those experiences. Reminder: Success leaves clues and we can learn from our mistakes.

Negative Thinking Traps

All or Nothing: You look at things in absolute, black-and-white categories. There are only victories and defeats. The glass is either completely full or it's empty.

Mental Filter: You dwell on the negatives and ignore the positives. It's similar to the way that one drop of food coloring in a large glass of water changes the color of the entire volume of water. Some are inclined to focus on the positives and ignore or deny any negatives.

Overgeneralization: You view a negative event as a never-ending pattern of defeat. The clue here is the prevalent use of "always" and "never" in your language. Also watch for the negative use of these absolute words: every, all, none, everything, nothing, anything, anyone, everyone, nobody.

Type 9: The Self-Erasing Negotiator

Wings
Type 8: The Self-Reliant Challenger
Type 1: The Self-Criticizing Reformer

Arrows

In stress mode, 9 resembles an unhealthy 6.
In growth mode, 9 resembles a healthy 3.

Center or Triad

Type Nines operate in the Body Triad. The common experienced emotion is anger. He largely takes in information based on feelings rather than facts while struggling for things to be made right. Nines ignore their anger, while Ones internalize it, and Eights outwardly express it.

Subtypes

Self-Preservation 9s: **The Serene Collector**
Finds comfort in collecting or savoring memories and experiences.

Sexual 9s: **The Unifying Partner**
Seeks deep unity in relationships, blending their identity with their partner's.

Social 9s: **The Harmonious Contributor**
Participates in communities, often as a peacekeeper or helper.

Time Orientation

Past: Nines ruminate about how their lives were both positive and negative in the past, feeling stuck and unable to alter negative patterns or improve the good ones. Since a Nine naturally tends to gaze in their personal rearview mirror, the growth challenge is being mindful and intentional in choosing to experience the present moment and to plan for future goals and needs.

Negative Thinking Traps

Emotional Reasoning: You give too much authority, too much credit to your feelings as a reliable informant on reality. This can be summarized as "I feel it therefore it is true."

Personalization: You completely blame yourself for something you weren't entirely responsible for. Or you blame other people and overlook ways that your own attitudes or actions might have contributed to the problem.

Labeling: You identify yourself by your shortcomings. Instead of saying, "I made a mistake," you tell yourself, "I'm a failure," "I'm a fool," "I'm so stupid," "I'm an idiot, or "I am a loser." You are inclined to label others as well.

14

SOME THOUGHTS ABOUT THE THREE EMOTIONS

You may wonder why the three primary emotions are only negative emotions. Why just fear, shame, and anger? Why aren't any of the emotions positive ones like gladness, optimism, or excitement?

The primary emotion listed for each Enneagram type is the emotion they are most likely to struggle with based on the Triad or Center their type resides in. Therefore, the emotional struggle lines up as follows:

Anger: Types, 1, 8, 9
Fear: Types 5, 6, 7
Shame: Types 2, 3, 4

I'd like to take just a moment and say something about these three emotions so we're on the same page in defining and identifying them.

Anger

Anger is a response to a perceived injustice. A perceived injustice may be any treatment that seems unfair and unkind. Examples include a false accusation, wrongful blame, being cheated, being betrayed, or being lied to. Perhaps I was forgotten, slighted, ignored, or passed over. Maybe I was threatened, mocked, insulted. I might believe that I was given too much responsibility, given insufficient resources or compensation, or not given credit and appreciation for my efforts. It's possible I was manipulated or conned. Perhaps I was verbally abused. Perhaps physically assaulted. The list goes on and on. But the common denominator is the feeling that there has been an injustice.

And note that our anger may rise up in response to believing another person (or group) has been unfairly treated.

Fear

Fear is a response to feeling unsafe, that your safety or security is at risk or is being threatened in some way. You might feel physically unsafe on a ladder 10 feet off the ground. Back on the ground you could feel emotionally unsafe in the argument you're having with your wife. Fear tells you to protect yourself in some form or fashion. Or you might feel a lack of security because of the economy, your job security, the crime rate in your community, or the nation's divisive political climate.

While fear and anxiety are often used interchangeably, there is a difference between the two. Anxiety is not just a double-dose of fear; it has a different source. Anxiety is usually the emotional stress response to A) feeling overwhelmed in the moment or B) anticipating negative events and negative consequences.

That first strain of anxiety sounds like, "There's too much to do. And I can't figure out why my laptop isn't working. I can't possibly get all this done by 3:30. I can't keep all these balls in the air and all these plates spinning!"

The other strain of anxiety is anticipatory. It sounds something like, "Oh my God, I dread tomorrow. I haven't prepared enough to give this speech. I'm gonna bomb. The audience is going to be thinking, "Seriously? We had to pay money to hear this?" And the conference host is gonna be so pissed off. It's going to be horrible. I'll definitely not be invited back to speak to this group again...ever. Plus, word will get around and I may not get invited to speak anywhere."

Is it possible to experience fear and one or both branches of anxiety? Yes, fear may run next door and ring anxiety's doorbell and vice versa. Fear and anxiety can co-exist and be felt simultaneously. Not fun.

Shame

Shame is not just a response to having done something you feel terrible about. Guilt and shame are not the same thing. Guilt says, "I did something bad." Shame says, "I'm a bad person." Healthy guilt has the potential to promote corrective actions. Shame immobilizes. Shame makes us retreat, hide, and fold up like a cheap lawn chair or even collapse in ourselves like an imploded building.

To use Dr. Brene Brown's definition, "Shame is the feeling that I'm flawed and am unworthy of love, respect, or belonging." While we certainly might feel a sense of shame because of a past or current behavior, the source of shame we're talking about here in the context of the Enneagram is two-fold.

Shame doesn't limit itself to regretting or feeling guilt over an action or behavior, rather it expands and covers you like a suffocating weighted wet blanket and declares that you are pervasively flawed, that you have more personal liabilities than assets, that you are an embarrassment, a waste of time, or even a burden to others.

I realize I may seem like I'm chasing a shame tangent here, but as a therapist I know how powerful and damaging shame is for men, and this may be the only opportunity I get to share this with you.

For men, depression and shame go together, and it doesn't matter which arrives first because the other will soon follow and link up. Secondly, men who feel suicidal as well as men who make suicide attempts are more likely to do so from a place of shame than from a place of loss and grief. The combination of feeling shame plus hopelessness is literally deadly.

The two primary sources of shame for men are related to the two primary imposed cultural criteria for masculinity: Strength and Success. As men, we are expected (and we expect ourselves) to be strong and successful. Therefore, the two sources of our shame are Weakness and Failure.

The Shame of Weakness: As men we are supposed to be physically and emotionally strong at all times. And depending upon your particular values, you may add to physical and emotional strength the requirement to display moral strength and spiritual strength.

The Shame of Failure: As boys, competence and success in what our parents and peers valued gave us a sense of being worthy of parental love and peer respect and belonging. If your parents placed a high value on academics, you believed you had to perform well in the classroom. If sports were very important to your Dad, you likely sought to make him proud of you through athletic achievement. If both academics and athletics (or another skill or hobby) were put on a pedestal, you likely felt some pressure to excel at both.

This next statement is cliché but mostly true. What strength and success means to a boy is getting injured on the field but not crying. It means getting up, brushing off the dirt, ignoring the pain, staying in the game, and scoring a touchdown. There's strength and success in a nutshell. And that's the message and expectation we internalize and take with us right into adulthood.

Do you remember Michael Jordan's famous "Flu Game?" In a pivotal Game 5 of the 1997 NBA Finals, despite flu, fever, chills, headache, nausea, and exhaustion, Jordan led his Bulls team to victory with 38 points, 7 rebounds, and 5 assists while playing all but 4 minutes of the game. Immediately after the game, teammate Scottie Pippen is seen holding Michael up and helping him shuffle off the court in a daze. That's what it means to be a real man, right? Be a wounded warrior. Be a hero. Just don't quit. And do not fail.

Whereas the boy's success was measured on report cards and scoreboards, as a man his success is now measured by his resume and his bank account. The successful adult male excels vocationally and financially. The guy who is struggling in his career and/or feels that his income and net assets are inadequate, is vulnerable to shame.

As men, we are susceptible to tying our worth to what we do for a living and how much of a living we are making doing it. Do you see how the feeling of being weak or feeling like a failure are shame traps? Do you see how different (and subtle) they are compared to experiencing shame over a sinful action or behavior pattern?

It is beyond the scope of this book to adequately address the antidotes to a man's shame, anger, or fear. Entire books are written on each emotion. I regularly counsel in-depth with men who feel stuck in just one of those emotions. Nevertheless, I still wanted to describe and explain some of those core negative emotions since they are mentioned in most studies of the Enneagram.

15

GUYS LIKE US

It is with some caution that we offer our roster of some well-known men (living, historical, and fictional) according to their likely Enneagram type. Our reason for caution is because we all need to be a little hesitant to type even the people we know well. We must remember that the Enneagram goes beyond just observable behavior and considers our motivations for those behaviors.

The hesitancy to type others applies even more to assessing casual acquaintances, and moreover to people we observe from a distance, especially public figures and celebrities.

So, our proposed roster is primarily for illustration and entertainment purposes. C'mon, isn't it fun to know which celebrities and historical figures share your birthday? Likewise, when we discover our Enneagram type there is a natural curiosity about who else is like us. It's fun and even encouraging to consider what well-known figures, both actual and fictional, may share some of our personality features.

Famous Male 1s: Steve Jobs, George Harrison, Jerry Seinfeld, Jack Shephard from *Lost*, Atticus Finch in *To Kill a Mockingbird*, Thanos from Marvel Comics, Dexter Morgan from *Dexter*

Famous Male 2s: Will Ferrell, Tim McGraw, Darius Rucker, Sean Maguire from *Good Will Hunting*, Danny Tanner from *Full House*, and Jake from State Farm.

Famous Male 3s: Michael Jordan, Paul McCartney, Arnold Schwarzenegger, Apollo Creed from the *Rocky* series, Don Draper from *Mad Men*, Tom Haverford from *Parks and Recreation*

Famous Male 4s: James Dean, John Lennon, Tim Burton, John Locke from *Lost*, Loki from Marvel Comics, Napoleon Dynamite

Famous Male 5s: Albert Einstein, Bill Gates, Stephen King, Doc Brown from the *Back to the Future* series, Sheldon Cooper from *The Big Bang Theory*, Walter White from *Breaking Bad*

Famous Male 6s: Sigmund Freud, Bear Grylls, George Carlin, Dwight Schrute from *The Office*, Lt. Nick "Goose" Bradshaw from *Top Gun*, and *John Wick*

Famous Male 7s: Robin Williams, Jimmy Buffet, Kenny Chesney, Ryan Reynolds, Kramer from *Seinfeld*, Zack Morris from *Saved by the Bell*, Michael Scott from *The Office*

Famous Male 8s: Muhammad Ali, Frank Sinatra, Joe Rogan, Pete "Maverick" Mitchell from *Top Gun*, Johnny Lawrence from *The Karate Kid* series/*Cobra Kai*, Dom Toretto from *The Fast and the Furious* series

Famous Male 9s: President Abraham Lincoln, Ringo Starr, Nate Bargatze, Luke Skywalker from the *Star Wars* series, Daniel LaRusso from *The Karate Kid* series/*Cobra Kai*, Jim Halpert from *The Office*

NICK SHELL & RAMON PRESSON

16

RECOMMENDED RESOURCES FOR FURTHER STUDY

BOOKS

These are some books that have been helpful to us in our own journeys of self-understanding. Most of them were engaged further in the writing of this book.

The Road Back to You: An Enneagram Journey of Self-Discovery by Ian Morgan Cron & Suzanne Stabile

The Story of You: An Enneagram Journey to Becoming Your True Self by Ian Morgan Cron

The Path Between Us: An Enneagram Journey to Healthy Relationships by Suzanne Stabile

The Journey Toward Wholeness: Enneagram Wisdom for Stress, Balance, and Transformation by Suzanne Stabile

Enneagram Empowerment: Discover Your Personality Type and Unlock Your Potential by Lauren Miltenberger

The Honest Enneagram by Sarahjane Case

King, Warrior, Magician, Lover: Rediscovering the Archetypes of the Mature Masculine by Robert Moore and Douglas Gillette

Take Care of Your Type: An Enneagram Guide to Self-Care by Christina Wilcox

What's Your Enneatype? An Essential Guide to the Enneagram: Understanding the Nine Personality Types for Personal Growth and Strengthened Relationships by Liz Carver & Josh Green

Men, Women, and Worthiness: The Experience of Shame and the Power of Being Enough by Brene Brown (this is in audiobook format only)

The Soul of Shame: Retelling the Stories We Believe About Ourselves by Curt Thompson, M.D.

TED TALKS

The Stranger Inside by Susan Olesek

You Are More Than Your Enneagram Type by Christopher Heuertz

PODCASTS

There are as many podcasts out there about the Enneagram as there are books. Here's our pick for the best two.

Typology hosted by Ian Morgan Cron

www.typologypodcast.com

Here you'll find an exceptional archive of interviews with well-known men and women of every Enneagram type and in every career field imaginable. It's well worth the search.

The Enneagram Journey hosted by Suzanne Stabile
www.TheEnneagramJourney.org/podcast

Suzanne Stabile is a longtime and highly respected researcher, writer, and teacher of the Enneagram. Here you will find an extensive library of 100+ episodes to choose from to aid further insight into your type (and your partner's type). Most episodes are an interview format similar to Typology with the occasional Q&A episode thrown in.

More by Nick Shell & Ramon Presson

Blog by Nick Shell
"Family Friendly Daddy Blog"
www.familyfriendlydaddyblog.com

Books by Ramon Presson
When Will My Life Not Suck? Authentic Hope for the Disillusioned
When Will My Life Not Suck? Authentic Hope for the Disillusioned (Teen Edition)
101 Conversation Starters for Couples (co-authored with Dr. Gary Chapman)
101 More Conversation Starters for Couples (co-authored with Dr. Gary Chapman)
101 Conversation Starters for Families (co-authored with Dr. Gary Chapman)
Coming Fall 2024: *Spooning with a Fork: How to Be a Couple*

For Counseling, Consulting, Speaking, and Interviews
www.ramonpressontherapy.com